Finding Official British Information

CHANDOS
INFORMATION PROFESSIONAL SERIES

Series Editor: Ruth Rikowski
(email: Rikowskigr@aol.com)

Chandos' new series of books is aimed at the busy information professional. They have been specially commissioned to provide the reader with an authoritative view of current thinking. They are designed to provide easy-to-read and (most importantly) practical coverage of topics that are of interest to librarians and other information professionals. If you would like a full listing of current and forthcoming titles, please visit www. chandospublishing.com or email wp@woodheadpublishing.com or telephone +44 (0) 1223 499140.

New authors: we are always pleased to receive ideas for new titles; if you would like to write a book for Chandos, please contact Dr Glyn Jones on email gjones@chandospublishing.com or telephone number +44 (0) 1993 848726.

Bulk orders: some organisations buy a number of copies of our books. If you are interested in doing this, we would be pleased to discuss a discount. Please contact on email wp@woodheadpublishing.com or telephone +44 (0) 1223 499140.

Finding Official British Information

Official publishing in the digital age

JANE INMAN
WITH CONTRIBUTIONS BY
HOWARD PICTON

CP
CHANDOS
PUBLISHING

Oxford Cambridge New Delhi

Chandos Publishing
Hexagon House
Avenue 4
Station Lane
Witney
Oxford OX28 4BN
UK
Tel: +44 (0) 1993 848726
Email: info@chandospublishing.com
www.chandospublishing.com

Chandos Publishing is an imprint of Woodhead Publishing Limited

Woodhead Publishing Limited
80 High Street
Sawston
Cambridge CB22 3HJ
UK
Tel: +44 (0) 1223 499140
Fax: +44 (0) 1223 832819
www.woodheadpublishing.com

First published in 2012

ISBN 978-1-84334-392-9 (print)
ISBN 978-1-78063-292-6 (online)

British Library Cataloguing-in-Publication Data.
A catalogue record for this book is available from the British Library.

Typeset by RefineCatch Limited, Bungay, Suffolk
Printed in the UK and USA.

Contents

List of abbreviations

ACAS	Advisory, Conciliation and Arbitration Service
ADAS	Agricultural Development and Advisory Service
AFA	Auxiliary Fire Service
ALGIS	Affiliation of Local Government Information Specialists (*part of* LARIA) (*www.algis.org.uk*)
AM	Assembly Member (Welsh Assembly)
APPSI	Advisory Panel on Public Sector Information (*www.appsi.gov.uk*)
AQMA	Air Quality Management Area
ASP	Act of the Scottish Parliament
BERR	Department for Business, Enterprise and Regulatory Reform (*predecessor of* Department for Business, Innovation and Skills (*www.bis.gov.uk*))
BIPRA	British-Irish Parliamentary Reporting Association (*www.bipra.org*)
BIS	Department for Business, Innovation and Skills (*www.bis.gov.uk*)
BNB	British National Bibliography
BOPCRIS	British Official Publications Collaborative Information Service
BSO	Business Statistics Office
BVPI	Best Value Performance Indicators
CAA	Comprehensive Area Assessment
CAS	Census Area Statistics

CILIP	Chartered Institute of Library and Information Professionals (*www.cilip.org.uk*)
CLIP	Central and Local Information Partnership
CML	Council of Mortgage Lenders
CNC	Civil Nuclear Constabulary
COI	Central Office of Information (*www.coi.gov.uk*)
CORE	Coordinated Online Record of Electors
COSLA	Convention
CPA	Comprehensive Performance Assessment
CPS	Centre for Policy Studies
CRP	City Region Plan
CSO	Central Statistical Office
DCLG	Department for Communities and Local Government (*www.communities.gov.uk*)
DCMS	Department for Culture, Media and Sport (*www.culture.gov.uk*)
DECC	Department of Energy and Climate Change
Defra	Department for Environment, Food and Rural Affairs (*www.defra.gov.uk*)
DETR	Department of the Environment, Transport and the Regions (*predecessor of* Department for Communities and Local Government, Department for Environment, Food and Rural Affairs *and* Department for Transport)
DfE	Department for Education
DfT	Department for Transport
DIUS	Department for Innovation, Universities and Skills
DMRB	*Design Manual for Roads and Bridges*
DOE	Department of the Environment
DTLR	Department of Transport, Local Government and the Regions (*predecessor of* Department of the Environment, Transport and the Regions)

DVLA	Driver and Vehicle Licensing Agency (*www.dvla.gov.uk*)
DWP	Department for Work and Pensions
EDM	Early Day Motion
EIR	Environmental Information Regulations 2004
ESD	Electronic Service Delivery
FAQs	Frequently Asked Questions
FOIA	Freedom of Information Act 2000
GDP	Gross Domestic Product
GIS	Geographical Information System
GLA	Greater London Authority (*www.london.gov.uk*)
GLC	Greater London Council
GOWA	Government of Wales Act 2006
GSS	Government Statistical Service
HC	House of Commons
HCA	Homes and Communities Agency (*www.homesandcommunities.co.uk*)
HCIO	House of Commons Information Office (*hcinfo@parliament.uk*)
HCP	House of Commons Papers
HCPP	House of Commons Parliamentary Papers
HL	House of Lords
HLIO	House of Lords Information Office (*hlinfo@parliament.uk*)
HMIC	Her Majesty's Inspectorate of Constabulary
HMSO	Her Majesty's Stationery Office (*now part of* The National Archives (*www.nationalarchives.gov.uk*))
HOWIS	Health of Wales Information Service
HPA	Health Protection Agency
HSCB	Health and Social Care Board (Northern Ireland)
HSE	Health and Safety Executive
IDeA	Improvement and Development Agency

IFLA	International Federation of Library Associations and Institutions (*www.ifla.org*)
IFTS	Information Fair Trader Scheme
IPSV	Integrated Public Sector Vocabulary
ISG	Information Services Group
JISC	Joint Information Systems Committee
KS	Key Statistics
LA	Local authority
LAA	Local Area Assessment
LACORS	Local Authority Coordinators of Regulatory Services
LARIA	Local Authority Research and Intelligence Association
LAWS	Local Authority Websites Project
LCC	London County Council
LCO	Legislative Competence Order
LDA	London Development Agency
LDP	Local Development Plan
LEP	Local Enterprise Partnership
LFEPA	London Fire and Emergency Planning Authority
LGA	Local Government Association
LGE	Local Government Employers
LGIU	Local Government Information Unit
LSC	Learning and Skills Council
LTP	Local Transport Plan
MCDHW	*Manual of Contract Documents for Highways Work*
MEP	Member of the European Parliament
MHRA	Medicines and Healthcare Products Regulatory Agency
MLA	Member of the Legislative Assembly (Northern Ireland)
MP	Member of Parliament (Westminster)

MPA	Metropolitan Police Authority
MSP	Member of the Scottish Parliament
NALC	National Association of Local Councils
NAO	National Audit Office
NDPB	Non-Departmental Public Body
NFER	National Foundation for Educational Research
NFS	National Fire Service
NHS	National Health Service
NISRA	Northern Ireland Statistics and Research Agency
NMD	Non-ministerial Department
NOMS	National Offender Management Service
OA	Output Area
ODPM	Office of the Deputy Prime Minister
Ofcom	Office of Communications
Ofsted	Office for Standards in Education, Children's Services and Skills
Ofwat	Water Services Regulation Authority
ONS	Office for National Statistics (*www.statistics.gov.uk*)
OPCS	Office of Population Censuses and Surveys
OPSI	Office of Public Sector Information (*now part of the* National Archives, *www.nationalarchives.gov.uk*)
PCT	Primary Care Trust
pdf	Portable Document Format
PGA	Public General Act
PITO	Police Information Technology Organisation
PLS	Public Library Subsidy
PM	Prime Minister
PMQ	Prime Minister's Question Time
PQ	Parliamentary Question
Quango	Quasi autonomous non-governmental organisation

RCUK   Research Councils UK
RDA   Regional Development Agency
RPI   Retail Price Index
RSL   Registered Social Landlord
RSS   Really Simple Syndication
SCD   Standing Committee Debates
SCOOP   Standing Committee of Official Publications
SCURL   Scottish Confederation of Universities and
           Research Libraries
SDP   Strategic Development Plan
SHA   Strategic Health Authority
SI   Statutory Instrument
SID   *Sessional Information Digest*
SIF   *Statutes in Force*
SIGLE   System for Information on Grey Literature
SLD   *Statute Law Database*
SNP   Scottish National Party
SOA   Single Outcome Agreement
SOCA   Serious and Organised Crime Agency
SOCITM   Society of Information Technology
           Management
SP   Scottish Parliament
SPICe   Scottish Parliament Information centre
SSI   Scottish Statutory Instrument
ST   Standard Tables
TfL   Transport for London
TRO   Traffic Regulation Order
TSO   The Stationery Office
UKAEA   United Kingdom Atomic Energy Authority
UKOP   United Kingdom Official Publications
           Database
UKSA   United Kingdom Statistics Authority
           (*www.statisticsauthority.gov.uk/*)
UKTI   UK Trade and Investment

UKWAC	UK Web Archiving Consortium
URL	Uniform Resource Locator
URN	Unique Reference Number
WALC	West Midlands Association of Local Councils
WHISP	What's Happening in the Scottish Parliament
WIB	*Weekly Information Bulletin*
Wiki	Hawaiian word for 'fast' and name for a collaborative website which can be edited by anyone who can access it
WPQs	Written Parliamentary Questions
XML	Extensible Markup Language

Preface

The aim of this book is to provide a reference guide to official publishing at a time when material published by public sector organisations is usually available in a digital form – on websites and via other technologies. Sometimes the digital version may be the only format as organisations look for ways of disseminating information more widely and economising on the costs of publishing information. The web is the place most people expect to find official information today, with nearly three-quarters of the population now having the skills and the technology to access information this way. However, we are a long way from being a paperless society and documents are still published in a traditional manner, possibly with print as the primary source but with an electronic version also available. This was, until very recently, the most common approach but the situation is changing rapidly, with print increasingly the spin-off version produced.

While the 'digital divide' still exists care must be taken to ensure that those without the skills and/or the technology have equality of access to official information. This is information we will all need at some stage in our lives as we access services or pay our taxes.

Keeping track of information in the three categories, i.e. print only, digital only and both forms, adds another level to what is already a complex area. The rapid changes in the available technology and moves to use more sophisticated applications such as social networking tools make this an area of constant change. This book can therefore only be a snapshot of current practice. The aim is to offer sufficient core information about the underlying structures and management of official information so that the book will be of use even as the sector changes. *Refer*, the journal of the Information Services Group (ISG) of the Chartered Institute of Library and Information Professionals (CILIP), provides regular updates on this area of information work. Extra information is available from the Referplus website at *http://sites.google.com/site/referplus/*. SCOOP, the Standing Committee on Official Publications, 'aims to improve access to and availability of UK official publications'. It is a forum which brings together librarians and information professionals with those responsible for the publication and dissemination of official publications such as The Stationery Office and HMSO. Its work over nearly 40 years has been effective in improving the way official information is made available both before what we are calling the digital age and since the explosion of digitally available information.

This book is not intended to be an academic discussion of the problems relating to official publications. It is designed to be a practical guide for those who need to access and manage official publications but who lack formal training in this area.

Acknowledgements

This book would have been an impossible task without the willing and patient support and advice of many people. We are particularly indebted to all our colleagues on the Standing Committee on Official Publications (SCOOP) whose expertise we have frequently drawn upon. We would especially thank Chris Pond, formerly Head of Reference Services, Department of the Library at the House of Commons, for checking and advising on the Parliamentary chapter, Alan Pawsey, formerly Head of Legislation and Publishing Services at the Office of Public Sector Information, now part of the National Archives, and Hannah Chandler, Official Publications Librarian at the Bodleian Library, Oxford.

We owe a huge debt of thanks to David Butcher, author of *Official Publications in Britain*, who has patiently read and re-read and advised on early drafts. Our thanks to Valerie Nurcombe, editor of *Information Sources in Official Publications* whose book we have relied upon, and to Alastair Allan, until recently the Chair of SCOOP, who never ceases to challenge the way official information is published.

George Woodman MBE, Librarian of the Northern Ireland Assembly, Francesca McGrath, Reference and Documentation Specialist at the Scottish Parliament Information Centre, Stephen Gregory, Legal and Business Librarian at the Welsh Assembly Government, and Robert Phillips, Accessions Librarian at the Legal Deposit Unit of the National Library of Wales, all helped immeasurably in providing advice and guidance on information published by the devolved assemblies.

Our thanks to Annabel Davis, former Head of Information Services at the GLA, and her team for help on information produced by the GLA, and Jennie Grimshaw, Social Sciences Librarian at the British Library, and her team for advice on electoral registers and other local authority information held by the British Library and for generally being very encouraging and supportive.

Dr Mike Anson, Historian at the Bank of England, and Dr Joe Ganley, Senior Analyst at the Bank, have encouraged and advised. David Sands, Housing Consultant, provided the case study on housing statistics used in the statistics chapter. The chapter on statistics would not have been possible without the help of SCOOP members who have held seminars on the topic, and Oscar Yau, a former statistician for the Department of Communities and Local Government, who developed the housing statistics section of its website in its current form. Our thanks also to the Committee of ALGIS and the Chair of LARIA, Andy Davis, who have been most supportive and to colleagues in the Customers and Communications Team in the Environment and Economy Directorate of Warwickshire County Council.

Last, but by no means least, our very grateful thanks to our long-suffering families who have lived with the book for far too long.

About the author

Jane Inman is a Fellow of the Chartered Institute of Library and Information Professionals and has worked in a number of different library sectors since qualifying as a Librarian in 1974. She has worked in public, academic, school and special libraries which has given her a breadth of experience. Most recently she has worked on the provision of an information service in a large local authority directorate within Warwickshire County Council. Jane has now moved into a wider role within the directorate managing a team with responsibility for public-facing communications through the web and printed material which involves advising on the directorate's approach to communicating with its customers. Responsibility for internal communications with staff through the intranet and briefings is also within her remit.

The team still provides an information service to the directorate which encompasses various aspects of information management and governance such as dealing with freedom of information requests and ensuring compliance with data protection legislation.

Jane was until recently Chair of the Affiliation of Local Government Information Specialists which formed part of LARIA (the Local Authority Research and Intelligence Association). It provided a network for people working with information in local government whether publishing, managing the increasing demands of freedom of information and related legislation or providing information for staff.

Jane writes regularly for various newsletters and journals, including CILIP's *Update*, and her articles cover the changes to and developments in the way in which information from public sector bodies is made available in this digital age.

She is a longstanding member of the Standing Committee on Official Publications, a forum for the users and publishers of official information which has made a substantial contribution over nearly 40 years to the way official information is made available. It provides an opportunity for librarians who collect, manage and use official information on behalf of their readers to work with the publishers of official information such as the National Archives and The Stationery Office. They work to ensure the best possible access to the information which all citizens need at some stage in their lives in order to access public sector services and to hold the government to account.

The author may be contacted at:

Jane Inman FCLIP
Customers and Communications Manager
Communities Group
Warwickshire County Council
Email: *janeinman@warwickshire.gov.uk*

The digital environment

What is the digital age?

> Was there really in any significant sense a Railway Age? If there was, when did it begin? Who was responsible for creating it? Has it left any permanent and recognizable mark on the landscape? Has human society been affected by it? Have politics and the map of the world been changed because of it? Is there something about the railway that made it characteristic of an age and significant above, or along with, other influences at work in its day? Are we still living in a railway age or has it ended?
>
> (Robbins, 1962)

There have been many publications referring to the 'digital age' but not many that choose to define the term. There have been various periods, dubbed 'ages', *after* the event (the space age being an exception), referring to periods when a particular innovation transformed society. Even now, arguments will rage over whether a particular 'age' ever existed, and when it began. And, if we have the temerity to attempt to label a period the 'digital age' before it seems hardly to have begun, we should bear Robbins' questions in mind. It appears to us that with regard to a digital age, we could answer affirmatively many of Robbins' questions.

So, for the purposes of this book, the 'digital age' will be defined as a period when digital technology proved capable of transforming all aspects of our society through computers, networking and communication devices. One might argue when precisely this 'age' began (with the invention of the computer? with the invention of the Internet? or when the Internet became a popular medium?) and obviously, we are only at the beginning of this 'age'. It would be rash to predict how long it may last (perhaps 'ages' are becoming shorter as innovation increases apace) but transformation of everyday life has already happened, particularly in the field of communication.

Digital availability has had a bigger impact on official publishing than in other areas because official publications were always, for the most part, little publicised and an unknown quantity to the general public. With the development of the Internet this has now changed and access is more widespread than before, although perhaps public understanding of the nature of official publications is no better than in the days of print.

With the first government websites appearing in 1995 we are still not 20 years into the digital age as far as official publications and information are concerned. Developments in the technology and its uses will continue to change the way we access official information but it is fair to say that the exploitation of the available technology has already had a substantial impact on the way we access and use official information.

E-government

Much of the drive to ensure that official information was made available electronically came in the form of e-government targets set by the government through the early part of the twenty-first century. Most of the targets focused on the provision of web-based information but the available technologies have now expanded so in any discussion of digital information sources we must now include digital TV and information provided through kiosks and plasma or LCD screens. Within this environment there are a number of other electronic tools which are being used to make information easier to access and use such as webcasts, podcasts, blogs and RSS feeds. It can be argued that call centres or customer service centres should be included here as they use electronic technology to communicate with the citizen and give access to information, and indeed the government included them within the definition of e-government.

The websites of official bodies have undergone numerous changes since they were first launched in the mid-1990s but many are still subject to criticism. Much of the drive now comes from the customer who has become used to 24-hour access to information and services from commercial organisations and is demanding the same level of service from local government, central government and other public bodies.

Beyond information – other services

Of course, websites do not just offer an alternative to publications but access to interactive services from official bodies as well. The Driver and Vehicle Licensing Agency (DVLA), for example, has had huge success with the introduction of online purchasing of car tax discs. Launched in January 2006, the service was being used by a third of vehicle owners within 18 months and at peak times handling as many as 86,000 hits a day. The service offers the vehicle owner the chance to purchase the tax disc online at their own convenience without the need to go to the Post Office and without being limited to normal Post Office opening hours.

This is not at first sight the concern of this book but the other major advantage of this particular service is that details of MOTs and insurance are checked electronically, removing the need to locate the paper copies. This is therefore an example of an innovative use of information brought together to provide an improved customer service.

Not only does this offer choice to the customer but, as Sir David Varney identified in his report *Service Transformation* in 2006, it is also a way for public sector organisations to make savings. *Putting the Frontline First: Smarter Government* issued by the Labour government towards the end of 2009 continued the theme of driving savings and community and citizen engagement and involvement through improved digital access to services and to information. The Coalition government has continued this process via its own Efficiency and Reform programme and Transparency Agenda.

The drive for the public sector to provide information and services electronically is not just that it is a better service for the customer but that it also saves the organisation money. Figures published by SOCITM (Society of Information Technology Management) show the relative costs of providing information and services as:

Face to face £7.20 per visit
Phone £2.90 per call
Web 0.32p per visitor

(SOCITM, *Insight* (January 2011))

The Coalition government announced in October 2010 that it intended to make 'online' the default model for access to some government services. Francis Maude MP in announcing this ambition pointed out that 96 per cent of 25–34 year olds are Internet users but only 13 per cent of Government contact with citizens is online.

Although those without the necessary skills and technology must not be overlooked, the increasing pressure across the public sector to show cost-savings and efficiency gains will inevitably mean that savings will be a driver for electronic delivery of information and services. If tackled properly, electronic provision can both show savings and improve customer service.

Web addresses or URLs

It would make life relatively simple if all websites of public sector organisations used the same domain name but this is not the case. Normally for central and local government the 'gov.uk' domain is used but Parliament has its own domain (Parliament.uk) as do the NHS (nhs.uk) and the police (police.uk). Some use is made of 'info' and 'net' domains. In Scotland the domain 'info' is also used, for example, by the Scottish Information Commissioner.

Naming conventions within the addresses vary too. In central government there are variations in the way in which the departmental name is represented in the 'gov.uk' URL. For instance, the Department for Environment, Food and Rural Affairs, *www.defra.gov.uk,* demonstrates the most common approach but the Department for Business, Innovation and Skills opted not to include an initial for 'department' and uses *www.bis.gov.uk.* The Department for Culture, Media and Sport has taken a completely different approach and uses *www.culture.gov.uk.* Similarly, the Department for

Communities and Local Government focuses on its work with communities by using *www.communities.gov.uk*. Other variations include the Department for Transport (*www.dft. gov.uk*) while the Department of Health uses *www.dh.gov.uk*.

Directgov

Directgov is a multi-channel service focused on the website at *www.direct.gov.uk* and is the digital means by which government provides information and services for the general public. Its vision is to ensure that by 2012 it is the primary online destination for the public to interact with government digitally and aims to provide consistent and accessible information. This requires all public-facing services to be moved onto Directgov and good progress is being made with a good spread of information available.

Directgov is the latest in a succession of attempts at a one-stop-shop for government information and was launched in 2004, replacing UK Online (2000–04) which in turn was preceded by open.gov. It was previously accountable to the Cabinet Office and Central Office of Information but moved to the Department for Work and Pensions in 2008 before moving back to the Cabinet Office after the Coalition government was established in 2010. The site will also be the first point of contact for local government information.

The quality of the site was discussed by the Public Accounts Committee in 2007 when the National Audit Office report *Government on the Internet* was being scrutinised. A briefing to the Public Accounts Committee in 2007 highlighted that nobody really knew how many government websites exist but the NAO's best estimate was around 2,500. The intention outlined by the Transformational Government programme was to close as many as possible of these and focus government information on Directgov (*www.direct.gov.uk*) for the citizen,

Business Link (*www.businesslink.gov.uk*) for the business community and NHS Choices for health information at *www.nhs.uk*. The Coalition government is committed to further reducing the number of government sites by 75 per cent with the focus being on the delivery of services.

Business Link

The Business Link website is the equivalent of Directgov for businesses, and is designed to bring together in one place all government information related to business. This includes information about finance, legislation as it impacts businesses, tax issues for businesses, health and safety and employment issues, the environment, business growth and overseas trade. As with Directgov the site links to local information but is operated on behalf of the government by HM Revenue and Customs.

NHS Choices

NHS Choices provides health information and information about accessing NHS services in England. For more information on official information in the area of health see Chapter 3.

E-government in local government

The e-government agenda for local government was set out in 2000 and local councils were required to meet a set of targets by the end of 2005. This was initially set at 2008 but was brought forward. By the end of 2005 local authorities had met, on average, 97 per cent of the targets and had spent £2bn with £700m of this funding supplied by central government (*SOCITM IT Trends in Local Government December 2005*).

The targets were not specific at first and in an attempt to manage and standardise them the Electronic Service Delivery (ESD) Toolkit was developed by local authority practitioners. This provided a way of recording progress against the targets but grew into a forum for the exchange of ideas and a store of information on standards and suppliers. The targets were measured using a Best Value Performance Indicator (BVPI) and the ESD Toolkit allowed local authorities to keep track of their progress (*www.esd.org.uk*).

Various national projects were established to help authorities deliver the requirements of e-government, with software and schemas developed to avoid duplication of effort. An example is the NOMAD Project which looked at mobile and flexible working.

Standard indexing and navigation

Part of the drive behind the e-government targets was to standardise the way local authority websites delivered information. The first local authority websites appeared in the early 1990s and the quality, style and content varied considerably. SOCITM began reviewing local authority websites in 1999 and their annual publication *Better Connected*, charts the progress of council websites. The categories they used to judge the sites ranged from 'promotional', which were sites which carried the most basic information about the authority, through 'content' and 'content plus', to 'transactional' where the citizen could interact with the authority, applying for and paying for services online.

Attempts were also made to standardise the navigation and indexing of local authority websites. A standard navigation was developed by the LAWS (Local Authority Websites) project and at about the same time work began on a thesaurus to improve the subject indexing of local authority websites (*www.laws-project.org.uk*). In time a number of lists were produced and, for use in the subject element of metadata, the Integrated Public Sector Vocabulary (IPSV). IPSV is for use on both local authority and central government websites and was later developed to include terms suitable for indexing information designed for internal use as might be found on an intranet or document and records management system. IPSV complies with ISO 2788 and BS8723, the standards for monolingual thesauri, and by 2006 was mandatory on all local authority websites. The lists can be found at *www.esd.org.uk*.

Beyond information

The targets for e-government in local government focused on the provision of information, which is what we are most concerned with here, but they also required authorities to look at ways of interacting with their residents by electronic means. This included the ability to apply for and pay for services on line. Examples of the services offered online are payment of council tax, booking of sports activities, submitting planning applications, reporting faults on the highway or streetlights which are faulty, renewing or ordering library books, and school admissions.

Take-up of these services once they were in place was the subject of a major campaign in 2006 and of further promotion through to 2008 but still needs work if the huge investment is to pay dividends. The current focus for local government is on access to services with a move to separate the corporate or organisational information from the services for customers.

The other major change in accessing local authority information has been in the links made to the central government website *www.direct.gov.uk*. Part of the e-government work required local authorities to provide a set of deep links to Directgov so that citizens could be directed to local authority information accessed through a postcode search.

Transformational government

As the deadline for e-government delivery was reached, the government published *Transformational Government Enabled by Technology* which set out the next steps required to achieve the delivery of public services through the use of technology to citizens and businesses.

The strategy was followed by an Implementation Plan and a Timetable for Change. The Timetable identifies three phases, taking us through to 2011 where the ambitious aim is described as 'boundaries between departments, between central and local government, and between public, private and voluntary sectors continue to be less important'.

T-gov, as it became known, intended to provide for:

- the transformation of public services for the benefit of citizens, businesses, taxpayers and front-line staff;
- the efficiency of the corporate services and infrastructure of government organisations, thus freeing resources for the front line;
- the steps necessary to achieve the effective delivery of technology for government.

In the local government arena, T-gov was a continuation of the e-government work. However, without government targets and funding it was inevitable that it would not achieve the same level of change as e-government. The need to work more efficiently in order to cut costs and the need to meet increasing customer expectations have proved to be the more powerful drivers of improvements in local authority websites.

Other public sector bodies

The requirements for the electronic delivery of services and information for other public sector bodies were not as formalised as those for central and local government. A website is, however, an essential tool in communicating their existence, role and functions for any organisation in the twenty-first century. We are now living in an age when we make judgements about the quality of an organisation by viewing its website. An out-of-date website will lead us to make a less than favourable judgement about the quality of the organisation as a whole.

Other technologies and communications methods

Other technologies beyond simple websites now abound and are increasingly used to deliver and share official information. They are also valuable tools for engaging the public in the democratic process. The speed with which they develop is astounding. It is said that it took 38 years from its invention for radio to reach 50 million people, only 13 years for TV to reach the same number but Facebook was being used by 100 million within nine months of its launch.

Web 2.0 and social networking tools

Research continues to look at how the government can best use the technologies known as Web 2.0 or social networking.

The web, from its very beginnings, has been about collaboration and these developing technologies offer new ways of facilitating collaboration, hosting communities and generally offering opportunities beyond just posting and viewing information.

An independent review of the ways in which central government could use this technology to improve citizen engagement was commissioned by the Ministry of Justice, undertaken by the Hansard Society and published as *Digital Dialogues* at *www.digitaldialogues.org.uk*. It looked at a number of case studies including an exercise by 10 Downing Street to map a debate stimulated by a lecture given by the then Prime Minister, Tony Blair, and a community set up by the Sustainable Development Commission Panel on Aviation.

Social networking tools which form the basis of, for example, *Facebook* and *Myspace* are increasingly used as a platform for the transfer of information between groups of people who share a common interest. These may be primarily social uses but there are numerous business-related uses for this sort of technology. Communities of practice can help people debate issues, share best practice and find answers to questions. In time, they are sure to be used in imaginative ways by public sector organisations. Hammersmith and Fulham Borough Council was the first council to use the video-sharing site *YouTube* to announce a reduction in its council tax. The Council posted a short pop video featuring Harry Hammersmith and the Flyovers singing a new version of the Status Quo hit 'Down Down'!

RSS feeds are available from many websites. RSS (Really Simple Syndication) allows people to receive feeds of information which can be used on websites, intranets, extranets or in personal RSS readers. In official publishing the Legislation website (*www.legislation.gov.uk*) operates an RSS feed which will alert you to new legislation. The BBC operates a number of RSS services allowing selection of relevant areas of news and information, as do the Parliament site and many local authority, regional and central government sites. Readers need to know enough to visit the website and set up the RSS feed but once this is done the information will be automatically selected and displayed, keeping you up to date with minimum effort.

Blogs are in common use and are used by individuals to provide a record of their actions, thoughts and opinions. MPs and local councillors have made use of these. David Cameron, as leader of the Conservative Party, used a blog with a web camera to allow us to see a day in the life of a politician.

Podcasts allow us to hear or see broadcast material we may otherwise have missed. They are offered in many areas of official information but probably are best known for their use by the BBC.

SMS texting is used by local authorities, for instance, to communicate information about school closures and to receive reports of faults on the highway.

TV coverage of the House of Commons debates began in 1989. However, the BBC's coverage of proceedings in Parliament with 'Today in Parliament' and 'Yesterday in Parliament' has been around for more than 60 years and is now available as a podcast. The Parliament Channel, accessible through satellite and digiboxes, covers both Chambers as well as Select Committees.

The Parliament Live TV site offers live and archived coverage of the public proceedings of both the House of Commons and the House of Lords and will be discussed in Chapter 3. As well as archives of proceedings on video and audio, the site also offers a set of short films about various areas of Parliament. The Scottish Parliament is covered by Holyrood TV. Televised coverage of Parliament, the devolved assemblies and the European Parliament has been brought together on the BBC Democracy Live site *www.bbc.co.uk/democracylive*.

Wikis are used to build a body of information collected through collaboration. Wiki is the Hawaiian word for 'fast' and it is the name for software which allows anyone who can access it to edit it. The most famous use of wiki software is the Wikipedia website but it is increasingly used to collect information. In the world of official information wiki technology is used on the National Archives website *www.nationalarchives.gov.uk* where it was introduced in 2007 to allow people to share information about using the archives. Called *Your Archives* it is a community where users of the National Archives can share with others what they have discovered while searching. Users can add articles or transcripts of documents which all add to the store of knowledge held by the National Archives. The content is clearly distinguished from the official information on the site and carries a disclaimer saying that the 'National Archives cannot vouch for the accuracy of information appearing in *Your Archives*'. As with the Wikipedia, the entries contain links to existing entries and users are encouraged to add content on the topics in a list of 'wanted pages'.

Leaflets

Almost all the organisations we discuss in this book produce leaflets that are of an ephemeral nature and bibliographically these can be impossible to trace. Probably the issues which surround this type of publishing are rather different from the digital access we have been discussing above. Access to the information they contain, while they are current, is clearly their primary value. This will be of some value for future research or perhaps to show the situation at a point in time but this may be limited.

The problem in the digital age is that in many cases the information is best delivered electronically where paper and printing costs are minimised and it is possible to ensure the latest information is stored only once, reducing the risk of distributing out-of-date information. When information is delivered electronically, though, it may not reach the people who need it and who may not have access to the necessary technology.

Michael Stuart of the FRILLS service writing in *Refer* in 2006 argues too that the leaflet, despite its drawbacks, is often 'good looking, short, easy to understand and can be picked up and taken home. They are handy for embarrassing subjects . . . and often multi-lingual'. There will always be a role for printed leaflets but alongside this it must be recognised that increasing numbers of the population would prefer to access information from the comfort of their own homes at their convenience.

Collections of printed leaflets can be time consuming to manage effectively. They need to be checked to ensure the latest version is in circulation and out-of-date information removed, and collections can take up large amounts of space in libraries and other public buildings. Estimating the numbers required for print runs can be difficult, and if information changes unexpectedly and a new version is required then there can be huge amounts of waste.

However, we still live in a digitally divided era where often it will be those who most need the information who are least likely to have digital access. We have seen a rapid transition to the digital environment but it will still be some time before we reach the point where all public sector information can be delivered only electronically. The Coalition government appointed Martha Lane Fox as the UK Digital Champion with a remit to encourage as many people as possible to go online, and to improve the convenience and efficiency of public services by driving online delivery.

Print to digital publishing

The move from print to digital publishing has caused some concerns as familiar printed volumes have disappeared, sometimes with little or no warning and often because electronic is seen as a way of saving costs. However, as reading complex or lengthy information on a screen is slower and can be more difficult than reading the printed word, what has happened is that printing and its cost has moved from the publisher to the customer. The user will print out the information so as to read it comfortably or take it away if, for instance, they are using a public library computer.

There are many examples of familiar publications which have been moved from print to digital-only publication and below are included just a few in order to highlight the issues this approach can raise.

Examples

The National Railway Timetable Policy Board announced in December 2006 that it had made the complete railway timetable for 23 train operating companies available online and would cease publication of the printed version by the end of 2007. Part of the reasoning behind this was that sales of the printed version had dropped in ten years from 134,000 to just 20,000. Clearly it is easier to search such a vast store of data electronically than in hard copy and it can be updated more frequently but for the customer it assumes access to the necessary technology. The complete timetable is available to download from the Network Rail site (as are sections thereof) but the full timetable is 3,180 pages and 71.2Mb so it would be a challenge to print off! Andrew Martin writing in the *Guardian* also pointed out that you lose the serendipity of looking up one destination and then seeing another you hadn't thought of! A later development is the Pocket Timetable Tool which allows you to create a timetable to meet your specific requirements and then download it as a pdf to print or store on your computer.

However, the National Rail Timetable is now published in two printed versions. TSO publish one version and another is produced by Middleton Press, an example of a publication which has returned to print alongside the electronic version.

The Monthly Bulletin of Indices for Formula Variation of Price, familiar to many working in construction as the Baxter Indices, has now become the *BIS Price Adjustment Formulae Indices Online* and is only available electronically. The indices are used to calculate the variation of price contracts in line with changes in the cost of labour, plant and materials. It is one publication in a set of three and all are now available in electronic form only.

Now published by BIS, the publicity for the move claimed the benefits of this approach as:

- immediate access to up-to-date information;
- all the information contained in the publications transferred to the online service;
- access to a greater amount of historic data than previously printed in each publication;
- data in machine readable format.

UK: Official Yearbook, the correct title of which is *The Official Yearbook of the United Kingdom of Great Britain and Northern Ireland*, was first published in the 1940s but it was known as *Britain – year* (e.g. *Britain – 1990*) and later became *UK 2002* until 2005 when publication ceased. The Office for National Statistics (ONS) was responsible for the publication which provided a picture of Britain, its government, economy and institutions in an attractive and accessible format. The digital replacement consists of data sets on the ONS website brought together under a link to the *UK Snapshot*. It is arguably easier to find a specific data set but the book was widely used and popular, and there is nothing which gives an overview of different aspects of the UK in the way that the publication did. In effect you are left with the raw data without the added value provided by the previous publication.

Digital divide

A digital divide still exists between those who have the tools and skills to access a range of technologies (and the web in particular) and those who do not. This situation is bound to continue for some time to come.

David Butcher, writing in the early 1990s, expressed concern that at that time information which had been publicly available in the 1980s was less readily available as it was issued to restricted groups. One example he quoted was agricultural advisory material from the Agricultural Development and Advisory Service which by the 1990s was only being issued to ADAS clients and colleges of agriculture.

Free advice had been key to the development of agriculture after the war but the Agriculture Act 1986 allowed the government to charge for this advice as a way of reducing public expenditure. The Campaign for the Protection of Rural England lobbied against this and elicited an assurance that free advice would be retained for 'public good', which covered areas such as diversification, conservation and pollution. However, financial constraints limited what ADAS was able to make available. By 1992 ADAS had become a 'next steps' agency and was eventually privatised.

Today the type of advice offered by ADAS is 'freely' available on the Defra website but there are still barriers to access. The barriers which remain are the need to have:

- Internet access for which there will normally be a charge from the ISP;
- access to the appropriate technology; and
- the skills needed to use the technology.

Access to the technology and the skills

Figures from *Internet Access: Households and Individuals 2009* published by the ONS show that 70 per cent or 18.31 million households in the UK have access to the Internet and 63 per cent or 16.5 million have a broadband connection. This means that the majority of the population now have access to the Internet. However, speaking at the 2009 National Digital Inclusion Conference, Baroness Andrews highlighted that of the 17 million people not on line, 6 million are socially and digitally excluded and these are some of our most vulnerable people. The 2008 DCLG report on digital exclusion (*Digital Inclusion: An Analysis of Social Disadvantage and the Information Society*) says 'To consider ICT deprivation as somehow less important than, for example, poor education, underestimates the pace, depth and scale of technological change and overlooks the way that different disadvantages can combine to deepen exclusion'.

The Labour government set itself the target of eliminating the digital divide by the end of its third term of office, in

2010. How this was to be achieved was set out in a strategy issued by the Prime Minister's Strategy Unit working with the then Department of Trade and Industry in 2005 with a review of progress in 2008 (*Connecting the UK: The Digital Strategy*).

Skills

Those without the skills to use the available technologies are at a distinct disadvantage. The divide between those with and those without the necessary skills to access and exploit new technologies is deepening as the web becomes the first point of contact for so many of us when seeking information or services from the public sector. Efforts are being made by the Government to address the skills deficit through the work of the UK Online Centres (*www.ukonlinecentres.com*) and the Race Online 2012 project led by Martha Lane Fox, the UK Digital Champion (*raceonline2012.org/*).

The web and other technologies are often used to reach the younger members of the population. This generation has grown up with the Internet and possesses the skills to be able to access it.

An interesting example of this is *Young Scot* which is the national youth information and citizenship agency for Scotland. The website for the agency *www.youngscot.org* carries information, news, links, competitions etc., all geared to the 12–26 year old age range. As well as the national site there are related sites for each of the Scottish local authorities. The body operates eRoadshows through vans equipped with laptops and a satellite dish which can be set up to provide a cyber café at schools, youth centres or shopping centres and provide sessions on relevant topics. The site makes extensive use of podcasts providing through this medium access to information on alcohol, writing CVs and interviews with MSPs (Members of the Scottish Parliament).

The Centre for Policy Studies (CPS) even claims that the Internet will change politics just as television changed politics in the twentieth century. CPS believes the Internet could be used to connect MPs directly with the concerns of their constituents.

References

Cabinet Office (2005) *Transformational government: Enabled by technology.* Cm 6683. London: TSO.

Cabinet Office (2007) *Transformational Government: Enabled by Technology – Annual Report 2006,* Cm 6970. Online at: *www.cio.gov.uk.*

Cabinet Office, Prime Minister's Strategy Unit with the Department of Trade and Industry (2005) *Connecting the UK: The Digital Strategy.* Online at: *www.cabinetoffice.gov.uk.*

Communities and Local Government (2008) *Digital Inclusion: An Analysis of Social Disadvantage and the Information Society.*

HM Government (2009) *Putting the Frontline First: Smarter Government* Cm 7753.

Martin, Andrew (2007) 'End of the line for railway timetables' *Guardian G2* 16 May.

National Audit Office (2007) *Government on the Internet: Progress in Delivering Information and Services Online,* Report by the Comptroller and Auditor General HC 529.

Office for National Statistics (2004) *UK 2005 The Official Yearbook of the United Kingdom of Great Britain and Northern Ireland.* Palgrave Macmillan online at: *www.statistics.gov.uk/yearbook*

Robbins, Michael (1962) *The Railway Age.* London: Routledge & Kegan Paul.

SOCITM *Better Connected*, annual review of local authority websites published from 1999 to present. *www.socitm. gov.uk*

Stuart, Michael (2006) 'Working with leaflets' *Refer*, 22(3): 16–20

Varney, Sir David (Chairman) (2006) *Service Transformation: A Better Service for Citizens and Businesses, a Better Deal for the Taxpayer*. London: HMSO/Treasury.

2

Definitions and why official information is published

Scope

What is an official publication?

A definition of an official publication was first agreed and published by the International Federation of Library Associations and Institutions (IFLA) in the 1980s. They stated that an official publication is 'any item, produced by reprographic or any other method, issued by an organisation that is an official body and available to an audience wider than that body'. The definition goes on to define official bodies as:

(i) any legislature of a state, or federation of states: or of a province, state, or regional, local or other administrative sub-division;

(ii) any executive agency of state, or federation of states; or of a province or state, or regional, local or other administrative sub-division;

(iii) any court or judicial organ;

(iv) any other organisation which was set up by an official body as in (i), (ii) and (iii) above, and maintains continuing links with that body whether through its reporting mechanism or accountability;

(v) any organisation of which the members belong to any of the four above categories, including intergovernmental organisations, provided that the body is considered to be official in the country concerned.

Using this definition, all information issued by a public sector organisation, which is intended for use beyond that organisation, is within the remit of the book and it will therefore exclude documents and information created only for internal use. However, much of the internal information produced by public sector organisations would now be required to be released under Freedom of Information legislation. Sensitive information not released under the Freedom of Information Act would be released under the twenty-year rule which will replace the thirty-year rule as a result of implementation of the changes brought about by the Constitutional Reform and Governance Act given Royal Assent in April 2010.

The information can be in any form from print to web content, from CD-ROM to leaflet and from digital TV to pdf. The issuing body is what makes it an official publication, not the published form or the subject matter covered, and the fact that a commercial publisher may be used to disseminate the information is irrelevant to this definition.

Organisations covered

To identify what constitutes a public sector organisation Schedule 1 to the Freedom of Information Act 2000 (FOIA) has been used as a basis. The Act identifies more than 100,000 'public authorities' in England, Wales and Northern Ireland which are required to comply with the legislation. These stretch from government departments, Parliament, the Northern Ireland Assembly and the National Assembly of

Wales through local government, the National Health Service, maintained schools and other educational institutions, the police and the numerous other public bodies and offices.

The schedules are updated as organisations cease to exist, are newly created or are identified as meeting the specification for being subject to the legislation. In 2010, for instance, The Freedom of Information (Additional Public Authorities) Order 2010 (SI 2010/937) added urban development corporations to Schedule 1 and The Freedom of Information (Removal of References to Public Authorities) Order 2010 (SI 2010/939) removed a number of bodies which had either ceased to exist or no longer satisfied the conditions for inclusion.

Public bodies are also listed in the Cabinet Office annual publication *Public Bodies* prepared by the Cabinet Office Agencies and Public Bodies Team and available at *www.civilservice.gov.uk/about/resources/public-bodies.aspx* along with earlier editions.

We add to this the public sector organisations covered by the Freedom of Information (Scotland) Act 2002 and the equivalent list of public bodies which in Scotland is issued by the Scottish Executive and called the *Scottish Public Bodies Directory* and which may be found at *www.scotland.gov.uk/Topics/Government/public-bodies/introduction*.

Details of government departments were taken from the *Civil Service Yearbook* which was published every each year and made available online as a subscription service. Publication of the *Civil Service Yearbook* has now ceased and information about staff in government departments is now published by the departments themselves on their websites and on the Prime Minister's Number 10 website *www.number10.gov.uk*. No longer having one point of reference for this information will make it more difficult to find, and ease of access will depend on the quality of the individual government department websites.

This makes it sound relatively straightforward to identify public sector bodies. Guidance issued for government departments on categorising public sector bodies, however, runs to some 33 pages! It is important that public bodies are accurately identified for accounting purposes and the Cabinet Office, HM Treasury and the Office for National Statistics are consulted to ensure consistency in the classification for the purposes of National Accounts and inclusion in the list of public bodies maintained by the Cabinet Office.

Public sector organisations in all areas are subject to change as needs and policies change but the changes generated by the election of the Coalition government in May 2010 have been more rapid and far reaching than those seen for a long time. This has made it doubly important to try to set down principles and direct readers to sources of information of the remaining organisations rather than write in specific terms.

There are now a number of websites which give access to official information but are not provided by official bodies, e.g. *www.theyworkforyou.com*, and the book will touch on these.

Geographical scope

The geographical scope of the book is limited to the United Kingdom (UK). The UK's full title is the 'United Kingdom of Great Britain and Northern Ireland' and Great Britain consists of England, Wales and Scotland. It was formed in 1801 as a result of the Act of Union 1800 and includes the large islands of Western Scotland, the Inner and Outer Hebrides and the northern isles of Orkney and Shetland, the Isle of Wight, Anglesey and the Isles of Scilly.

For information on the official publications of other countries beyond the scope of this book we would recommend *Information Sources in Official Publications*. Although this is more than ten years old it is still a useful guide to official publications on the international stage.

Published formats

The book focuses on digital publishing but not exclusively so, and clearly much of this has its roots in printed material. So, for instance, it will look at retrieving information which was published regularly and issued in hard copy but is now perhaps being issued only as an electronic document on a website. There are many instances of this approach but there are also areas of information which have no printed ancestry and, of course, there are many publications which appear in both forms. Older material will almost certainly be available only in print, making comparisons difficult, for instance, when using statistical information. Digital information chiefly refers to information made available on the Internet but includes, as far as is possible, the material which is produced digitally for distribution using other means such as digital TV.

To cover all publications would be an impossible task. Instead, principles are set down and practical examples given which help build an understanding of this area of publishing. Although the primary focus is current material, details of specialist collections of historical papers are included as appropriate. In particular there is coverage of those which are the subject of digitisation projects and are becoming easier to access.

In covering the output of Parliament the legislative process is addressed but the intention is not that this book be a guide to legal information sources. This topic has been covered by David Pester in *Finding Legal Information: A Guide to Electronic Sources* (2003). *Legislation.gov.uk*, which is described as the 'official home of UK legislation', is covered as is the Parliamentary process by which our laws are made.

Structure

The book is divided into chapters on broad groups of public sector organisations, e.g. Parliament, central government. In each area there is an introduction to the structure and function of that group of public sector organisations, a description of the main areas of publishing for which they are responsible, examples of publications and assistance in tracing them through bibliographic tools and alerting services. The book works from the national to the local, so begins with the UK Parliament, the devolved assemblies and central government departments, other public sector bodies, regional bodies and local government. Along the way it encompasses regulatory bodies, government and specialist agencies, research councils, the NHS and much more.

The book includes a look at the specific topic of statistics as this covers all areas and deserves a chapter of its own. Statistics are issued by public bodies in all the sectors covered by the book and they are in a unique position when it comes to collecting and publishing statistics. The issues around their publication, availability and accessibility are quite specific so require special consideration.

The legislative framework which governs official publishing and the digital environment will be described.

Why are we doing this?

What constitutes a public sector organisation covers more than 100,000 organisations. Clearly not all of them publish information although, of course, they all hold information, which they could, if they chose, publish and which they would have to supply on request under the requirements of FOIA. Taking just what *is* published represents a treasure store of information which is produced at public expense and which contributes to the knowledge base of the UK. This information includes everything from the *Radio Times*, published by the BBC, which it is easy to forget is a public body, to NHS leaflets on giving up smoking, council minutes for local authorities, traffic information from the Highways Agency, central government reports, legislation and *Hansard*, the official record of the proceedings of Parliament.

The aim is to help you exploit official publications as a source of information – a valuable resource that can often be overlooked. Official publications are often seen as difficult and inaccessible, perhaps because of the scale of the publishing involved, the number and variety of organisations issuing material and the breadth of topics covered. They may not always make the headlines although they include some very high-profile reports such as those published after inquiries and reviews, e.g. the Stephen Lawrence Inquiry (*Report of an Inquiry by Sir William Macpherson of Cluny*, Cm 4262-1, 1999) or the Shipman Inquiry into the murders committed by Dr Harold Shipman which was completed in 2005 (*Shipman Inquiry*, Chairman Dame Janet Smith DBE, *www.the-shipman-inquiry.org.uk*). They may not always sell in huge numbers but again some prove surprisingly popular. Andrew Marr, in *A History of Modern Britain*, describes the 1942 publication of the Beveridge Report on the creation of a welfare state and how it sold 100,000 copies in the first month. It eventually sold 600,000, 'was distributed to British Troops, snapped up in America and dropped by Lancaster bombers over occupied Europe as propaganda'.

It is always difficult to put a value on information but being unaware of the content of official publishing could cost an organisation dear. A report by the Office of Fair Trading (*The Commercial Use of Public Information*) issued in December 2006 estimated that with improvements to the way public sector information is handled, the contribution it makes to the UK economy could be as much as £1bn annually. After all, in many cases the public sector will be the only source of that information. For example, in more practical terms, to run a successful business demographic information is often key and can be obtained from the Office for National Statistics (ONS). Collecting a fraction of the data collected by ONS would be an expensive exercise. ONS itself has a budget of £195m to carry out this function on behalf of the country while the budget for the 2011 Census is £482m (*Hansard*, 15 May 2009, col. 1047W). However, it is estimated that the value to the economy of the information which this exercise will produce is in the region of £700m.

Similarly, local authorities produce economic profiles of an area which can provide useful information to businesses planning to relocate and could save them a great deal in research costs.

Another reason for covering this topic is that it is now rarely taught on information courses so many newly qualified information workers may have little understanding of official publications. In order to survive in the information world some understanding of this area of publishing is essential.

Why not just use Google?

Often Google *is* all you need if you know what you are looking for. Finding a government report when you know the title or have some idea of the subject matter or issuing body is easy with Google or other search engines. The quality of individual search engines on government and local government websites still means that often this is a better way of finding information than through the site itself. This is certainly suggested as a quick way to find much of what is published but it only really works if you know the information exists digitally or have some idea it may.

However, it must be remembered that even though Google is the search engine of choice for many people and the results it delivers are impressive there is still much that it doesn't find or display. With in excess of 51 billion pages now on the web, the number that Google indexes is only in the region of 16 billion, leaving vast quantities of material which are not indexed and won't be revealed by a search using Google or, for that matter, an alternative search engine. Even if they are identified by a search engine it is possible they will not appear in the first page or so of results and users may not go far enough in checking those results.

An awareness of what exists is vital if you are to make the most of official publishing. If you do not know what official information is issued on a topic or if you are undertaking detailed research, then you need more than Google. As part of this, some understanding of the structure and functions of the plethora of public sector organisations and their published output is essential.

Keeping track of official publications was never easy but there was a time when the majority were published by a single government publisher, Her Majesty's Stationery Office (HMSO) and this was funded by the HMSO Vote so that central government departments did not have to pay for the publishing. Since the 1980s when first HMSO became a trading fund and then departments were allowed to take their business elsewhere this has changed, making the tracking of official publications more complex. In fact even before this time publishing had begun to move away from HMSO, with a period in the 1960s in particular when little was published by HMSO. Outside of central government there has always been a substantial amount which has never been handled by HMSO, e.g. local authority publications.

Why public sector bodies publish information

Central and local government and other public bodies have a duty to ensure they make information available to the public for a variety of reasons. This duty may be enshrined in legislation or may be implicit within a particular duty or function. It is also, of course, the taxpayer who has funded research and other work undertaken by public sector organisations and who should, it is argued, be able to see the results of that investment. It is essential that citizens are able to access the information they need to enable them to be engaged in the government of their country, to hold the government to account and to form their opinions on the basis of the facts.

An example at a local and practical level is the Road Traffic Regulation Act 1984 which lays down how the public are to be notified of plans by the highway authority to close a road, apply parking restrictions, impose speed limits or set weight restrictions etc. The proposed changes are made through a Traffic Regulation Order (TRO) and before these can be enforced the process requires that the public be made aware of them through notices published in local papers and on site.

Similar requirements are placed on local authorities to make the public aware of planning activities and these are looked at in more detail in Chapter 7 on local government.

Requirements are also placed on bodies such as the NHS (National Health Service) to ensure the public are aware, for instance, of certain public health issues. With the introduction of more choice for patients, information is essential if an informed decision is to be made.

It is fundamental to democracy that the government communicate with the public both to consult and to inform. In 2003 the Public Administration Select Committee recognised that a review of government communications was needed in the wake of the resignations of Jo Moore and Martin Sixsmith from the then Department of Transport, Local Government and the Regions (DTLR) over accusations of burying bad news. The Phillis Report which followed identified a breakdown in trust between the government and politicians, the media and the general public. Among its recommendations were improvements to government websites and to the way the government structures the communication functions across government and in the departments, ensures civil servants' impartiality and briefs the media.

There are times, of course, when the government needs not only to make information available but also to positively promote certain messages. As far back as the mid-nineteenth century a dedicated publicity unit was set up as part of the Post Office and ran its first campaign in 1876 using a million handbills to promote the benefits of government savings schemes. From these early beginnings the Central Office of Information (COI) emerged in 1946 and is still in place today to provide the government with marketing and communications expertise. It operates a News Distribution Service which manages news releases for Whitehall departments and other agencies and non-departmental public bodies and anyone can register to receive emails from the website *http://nds.coi.gov.uk*. Since the election of the Coalition government there has been a freeze on non-essential government marketing and advertising and the COI is considerably reduced in size.

Legislation

There is much legislation which governs what information public sector organisations should publish such as the Road Traffic Regulation Act mentioned above. Very often the legislation concerns a specific topic and the publication of information is only a very minor part of the duty placed upon a public sector body by the Act. However, there are a number of Acts which are specifically about the duties of public sector bodies to make information available and in this way to contribute to the transparency and accountability of the public sector. The most important of these and the one which has had the greatest impact is the Freedom of Information Act 2000 (FOIA) together with the Freedom of Information (Scotland) Act 2002.

Freedom of information

The Act, which has been in force since 1 January 2005, covers more than 100,000 public sector organisations in England, Wales and Northern Ireland, who are required to provide information to anybody submitting a request.

Requests must be in writing and public sector organisations must respond within 20 working days of the request being received. The Act was fully retrospective so covers all information held by a public body and anyone is entitled to request information. There are a few 'exemptions' which prevent the release, for instance, of information which might be prejudicial to national security, personal information which is covered by data protection legislation, information already publicly available or information the release of which could adversely affect the conduct of public affairs.

Probably the most high-profile use of the legislation has been in the area of MPs' expenses at Westminster. The impact of the information published in this situation has been far reaching, leading to fundamental reviews and changes in the way the process works and even prison sentences for those whose mis-use of the system was exposed by the release of the information. The primary aim of the Information Commissioner in England and Wales is to 'bring about a culture where public bodies make as much official and environmental information available as possible, proactively and progressively with individuals widely aware of their right to know'. The Act is intended to improve transparency which in turn brings greater trust in public bodies. The Information Commissioner publishes a report at the end of each year and in the report for 2008/09, the fourth year of the FOIA being in force, survey results showed an increase in people believing that the Act increases confidence in public authorities from 51 per cent in 2004 to 84 per cent by 2008.

It is certainly the legislation that has done most to improve the availability of public sector information. For detailed information on the Act see the website of the Information Commissioner at *www.ico.gov.uk*.

The Scottish legislation is similar (Freedom of Information (Scotland) Act 2002) and came in to force at the same time. It is administered by the Scottish Information Commissioner and there is further information and guidance etc. at *www.itspublicknowledge.info*.

Publication schemes

As part of the legislation public bodies are required to produce a publication scheme. These are not designed to identify individual publications but categories of publications which that public body is committed to making available to the public. In effect they provide a framework within which a public body can work to ensure it makes information available consistently.

In practice it seems these schemes have not been as well used or as valuable as intended but they should not be overlooked. They are a statutory requirement and provide an overview of the published output of a public body. Each public body is required to make them available on their website and models were provided for different types of public sector bodies from 2008 which helps bring some consistency.

Environmental Information Regulations

Although originally issued in 1992 the Environmental Information Regulations (EIRs) were re-issued in 2004 to bring them in to line with the FOIA (Environmental Information Regulations 2004 SI 2004/3391) and Environmental Information (Scotland) Regulations 2004 (SSI 2004/520).

As with the FOIA they make provision for people to request information and they also make it a statutory requirement to make some environmental information available proactively. In this context 'environmental' is defined in very broad terms and therefore covers large amounts of information and data.

More organisations are covered by the EIRs than are included in the FOIA. This is because the legislation needed to be in line with the EC Directive on public access to environmental information (2003/4/EC) which included public utilities such as water, waste and energy, which in the UK are services now provided by private companies.

The regulations require a public authority to make environmental information which it holds 'available to the public by electronic means which are readily accessible and take reasonable steps to organise the information relevant to its functions with a view to the active and systematic dissemination to the public of the information'. (Information collected before 2005 in non-electronic form is excluded from this requirement.) The intention is to make sure the public are fully aware of any actions which could damage the environment and of the current condition of the environment such as air quality. Given the breadth of the definition of 'environmental' in this context the requirement is a substantial one and it may be argued that it is not being fulfilled as fully as the legislation requires. If compliance with this legislation was improved, vast quantities of environmental information would be made available which currently are not.

The Re-use of Public Sector Information Regulations

An EU Directive issued in 2003 led to the introduction of the Re-use of Public Sector Information Regulations SI 2005/1515 in July 2005. At the same time the Office of Public Sector Information (OPSI) was formed with the job of promoting the re-use of public sector information and finding ways of tapping into this valuable resource which at the time was estimated to be worth £590m (figures from the Office of Fair Trading).

At its inception OPSI was charged with promoting the re-use of public sector information and to tackle this it published guidance, introduced the Information Fair Trader Scheme (IFTS) and extended the Click-Use Licensing scheme originally introduced by HMSO for Crown Copyright material, in an attempt to simplify re-use of official information. In 2010 Click-Use was replaced with the Open Government Licence which aims to make it even easier to 'copy, publish, distribute and transmit information, adapt information and exploit information commercially, by combining it with other information, or by including it in your own product or application'. There are only limited restrictions with a requirement to:

- ensure that you do not use the information in a way that suggests any official status or that the information provider endorses you or your use of the information;

- ensure that you do not mislead others or misrepresent the information or its source;

- ensure that your use of the information does not breach the Data Protection Act 1998 or the Privacy and Electronic Communications (EC Directive) Regulations 2003.

Guidance appears on the National Archives website at *www.nationalarchives.gov.uk.*

Advisory Panel on Public Sector Information (APPSI)

The Advisory Panel on Public Sector Information (*www. appsi.gov.uk*) is a non-departmental public body of the

Ministry of Justice established in 2003 to 'advise ministers on how to encourage and create opportunities in the information industry for greater re-use of government information'. APPSI also has a role to review complaints under the Re-use of Public Sector Information Regulations and to advise the Director of the Office for Public Sector Information on 'changes and opportunities in the information industry'. APPSI was previously known as the Advisory Panel on Crown Copyright.

Legal deposit

Ensuring that what is published is preserved for future generations is the responsibility of the British Library and the other copyright libraries:

- Bodleian Library, Oxford (*www.bodley.ox.ac.uk*)
- University Library, Cambridge (*www.lib.cam.ac.uk*)
- National Library of Scotland (*www.nls.uk*)
- Library of Trinity College, Dublin (*www.tcd.ie/Library*)
- National Library of Wales (*www.llgc.org.uk/*).

The Copyright Acts 1911 and 1963, superseded by the Legal Deposit Libraries Act 2003 and the Copyright and Related Rights Regulations 2003, require all publishers and distributers in the United Kingdom and the Republic of Ireland to deposit a copy of each of their publications with the British Library. Items deposited under the legislation are then preserved for future generations and some are recorded in the British National Bibliography (BNB) and in the catalogues of the receiving libraries. BNB records much of the published output of the United Kingdom and the Republic of Ireland, both printed and electronic, and has been in existence since 1950. The Legal Deposit Libraries Act 2003 provides for regulations to be made to include the deposit of non-print material. Until legislation is in place the British Library encourages voluntary deposit.

At the beginning of March 2010 the Department for Culture, Media and Sport (DCMS) and the Department for Business, Innovation and Skills (BIS) completed a public consultation, based on recommendations from the Legal Deposit Advisory Panel, on the legal deposit of offline publications and online publications which are available free of charge and without access restrictions. Following that consultation, the DCMS in September 2010 produced for consultation a set of draft Regulations, Guidance and Impact Assessments for the legal deposit of non-print works. Subject to the outcome of this consultation they will submit these to Parliament for approval during 2011.

To keep track of progress in this area see the British Library website and follow the links from 'About us' to 'Strategies, policies and programmes' and then to 'Legal Deposit', at *www.bl.uk/aboutus/stratpolprog/legaldep*. You will also find guidance here on what should be deposited.

Data Protection Act 1998

The Data Protection Act gives individuals the right of access to information about themselves which is held by an organisation, and sets out how personal information should be collected, stored and processed. It is not strictly about publishing but is included here for completeness because it governs access to information, albeit personal information. It must be taken into account when information is published as it limits what personal information may be made publicly available and the information which can be released under FOIA. Data protection legislation only applies to living individuals which is why access to census records is permitted after 100 years or slightly earlier as has been the case with the 1911 Census in England.

The Information Commissioner is responsible for the administration of this legislation and has issued guidance both for the public and for professionals working in this area.

The large-scale losses of government-held personal data reported in 2007 and 2008 led to a renewed interest in and concern about the protection of personal data. The report of the House of Commons Justice Committee into the protection of private data found that the law needed to be strengthened and thought given to managing extensive databases where access is given to large numbers of officials (*Protection of Private Data*, First Report of Session 2007–08 (2008), House of Commons Justice Committee, HC 154).

Local Government Act 1972, Local Government (Access to Information) Act 1985 and the Local Government Act 2000

The Local Government Acts of 1972, 1985 and 2000 each added to the information which local authorities are required to make available and each was designed to increase the openness and accountability of local authorities. It is this legislation which requires local authorities to make committee papers available to the public five days before a meeting and which ensures that details of the decisions made are accessible.

Public Library Access Scheme

Although not a legislative measure, this seems the most appropriate place to include mention of the Public Libraries'

Access Scheme operated by the Office for Public Sector Information (OPSI). The Scheme replaced the Public Library Subsidy (PLS) in 2005 which provided a subsidy to all local authority-funded public libraries on official publications in order to support public access. The scheme now covers Parliamentary and government materials, and legislation not available on the official legislation website at *www. legislation.gov.uk*.

The funding released by the changes to the scheme is used to develop and improve the legislation web services originally provided on the OPSI website but now by *www.legislation. gov.uk*, and the consultation showed support for this approach.

The annual bound volumes of Public General Acts, Acts of the Scottish Parliament and Annual Editions of Statutory Instruments, Scottish Statutory Instruments, the Chronological Tables of the Statutes and the various Northern Ireland Annual Statutory Publications still attract a 50 per cent subsidy in recognition of the additional editorial features they contain. All local authority-funded public libraries are entitled to claim under the scheme and the publications covered are:

- Parliamentary and government materials;
- electronic publications (e.g. CD-ROM and online services) produced under Crown or Parliamentary copyright;
- printed books and electronic publications issued on behalf of:
  - the Audit Commission
  - the Competition Commission
  - the Environment Agency
  - the Legal Services Commission
  - official legislation not available online.

The scheme currently includes the FRILLS leaflet service and is regularly reviewed.

The scheme, as it was originally conceived and operated, encouraged widespread availability of official publications in public and other libraries throughout the country in print form. Because the funding has been reduced and the publications within its scope are now limited, this has inevitably reduced the availability of printed official publications in public libraries. There are improvements to electronic publication of the information but this does not help, for instance, public libraries without the facilities or the funding to print documents for use by readers unable to manage the information on the screen.

References

Note: Legislation is available on the Official Legislation website at *www.legislation.gov.uk* and is not listed here.

Cabinet Office (2005) *Classification of Public Bodies: Guidance for Departments*. Online at: *www.cabinetoffice.gov.uk*.

Cabinet Office, Agencies and Public Bodies Team (2009) *Public Bodies 2009*. Online at: *www.civilservice.gov.uk*.

Campaign for Freedom of Information. Launched in 1984 the Campaign for Freedom of Information led to the movement and the history of the legislation can be traced through the articles in the campaign's newspaper *Secrets* which can be accessed online at: *www.cfoi.org.uk/secrets. html*. *Note*: This is not an official source.

European Parliament. *Directive 2003/4/EC of the European Parliament and of the Council of 28 January 2003 on Public Access to Environmental Information and Repealing Council Directive 90/313/EEC*. Online at: *eur-lex.europa.eu*.

European Parliament. *Directive 2003/98/EC of the European Parliament and of the Council of 17*

November 2003 on the Re-use of Public Sector Information. Online at: *eur-lex.europa.eu*

Freedom of Information Act 2000: Designation of Additional Public Authorities. Online at: *www.justice.gov.uk/docs/cp2707.pdf.*

House of Commons Justice Committee (2008) *Protection of Private Data*, First Report of Session 2007–08, HC 154. Online at: *www.Parliament.uk.*

International Federation of Library Associations and Institutions, Official Publications Section (1983) *Proceedings of International Conference of Government Publishers, Printers, Librarians and Users, Saratoga Springs, New York, August 29–September 1, 1982*, eds B. Hoduski and M. Trautman. Washington, DC: IFLA, p.3.

McKay, Sir William, Cranmer, Frank, Hutton, Mark, Patrick, Simon, Robertson, Mary, Sandell, Alan (2004) *Erskine May: A Practical Treatise on the Law, Privileges, Proceedings and Usage of Parliament*, otherwise known as *Parliamentary Practice*, 23rd edn. London: Butterworths.

Marr, Andrew (2007) *A History of Modern Britain* Basingstoke: Macmillian.

Ministry of Justice (2007) *Freedom of Information Act 2000: Designation of Additional Public Authorities*, Consultation Paper CP 27/07. Online at: *www.justice.gov.uk.*

Nurcombe, Valerie J. (ed.) (1997) *Information Sources in Official Publications*. London: Bowker Saur.

Office of Fair Trading (2006) *The Commercial Use of Public Information* (CUPI), OFT 861.

Office of Public Sector Information (2007) *The United Kingdom Implementation of the European Directive on the Re-use of Public Sector Information – The First Two Years*. London: OPSI.

Pester, David (2003) *Finding Legal Information. A Guide to Electronic Sources.* Oxford: Chandos.

Phillis, Bob (Chairman) (2004) *An Independent Review of Government Communications Presented to the Minister for the Cabinet Office.*

Refer, Journal of the Information Services Group of the Chartered Institute of Library and Information Professionals. Online at: *www.cilip.org* and follow the links to special interest groups and Referplus (*http://sites.google.com/site/referplus*).

3

Parliament at Westminster

This chapter covers:

- the structure and role of the UK Parliament;
- Parliamentary business and procedures;
- the legislative process including the European Parliament and Westminster;
- visiting Parliament;
- key Parliamentary information resources.

Structure and role of the UK Parliament

Parliament is the UK's supreme legislative body and it comprises

- the House of Commons
- the House of Lords
- the Crown.

There is no written constitution for Parliament and the current system has evolved over some 800 years. Indeed, it has been pointed out that Britain is unique in having had a Parliament for hundreds of years before it had a democracy.

The UK Parliament has four main roles as it:

- enables government to raise the taxation needed to provide for its programme of work;
- scrutinises the work of the government and its departments;
- develops, debates and passes laws;
- provides a forum for debate on a wide range of issues.

The information which Parliament at Westminster publishes is therefore vital to the citizens of the UK. It is in this body of information that they find the laws of the land in which they live, can see the government held to account for its policies and decisions and see how their elected representatives have raised concerns on their behalf, although there is much debate on how well this is done.

House of Commons

There are 650 elected representatives – Members of Parliament (MPs) – in the House of Commons. There were 659 but this was reduced by boundary changes at the 2005 General Election when the number of Scottish MPs was cut as part of the outcome of the devolution settlement in Scotland.

Apart from Labour, Conservative and the Liberal Democrats, there are a number of other political parties with MPs at Westminster including the Green Party, nationalists (Scottish National Party and Plaid Cymru), and parties from Northern Ireland. There are also a few independent MPs. The party (or occasionally parties, if a coalition is formed as in May 2010) with a majority of seats in the Commons forms the government and implements its policies through legislation or other means while it is in office.

The role of the House of Commons is to debate important political issues and to propose and debate new laws. It has sole responsibility for making decisions on financial bills such as proposed new taxes.

An essential part of the role of an MP is to hold the government to account. They can do this for example by putting down Parliamentary Questions (PQs) to a minister which will then receive a response either orally in the Chamber or through written answers. MPs can also initiate debates either in the Chamber or in Westminster Hall, although most Parliamentary time is allocated to government business. A principal means of holding government to account is (or should be) via select committees (see below).

House of Lords

The House of Lords consists of 738 members (as at 1 November 2010) comprising Lords Spiritual (archbishops and bishops), life peers under the Life Peerages Act 1958, life peers under the Appellate Jurisdiction Act 1876 (judicial life peers) and peers under the House of Lords Act 1999. By the terms of the House of Lords Act 1999, most hereditary peers were required to leave the House. However, 92 remained, 90 as part of the agreement between the government and opposition and two because they hold hereditary royal appointments. Aside from the Lords Spiritual, there are Conservative, Labour and Liberal Democrat peers and crossbench and independent peers.

The role of the House of Lords, the second chamber, is to play an important

'part in revising legislation and keeping a check on government by scrutinising its activities. It complements the work of the House of Commons whose members are elected to represent their constituents. Members of the Lords are not elected and are unpaid although they receive an attendance allowance for each day that they attend the House. They have a wide range of experience and provide a source of independent expertise.'

(Extract from *House of Lords Briefing*, 2009)

It spends 40 per cent of its time scrutinising the work of the government through debate, questions and statements and 60 per cent working on legislation, of which 55 per cent is spent on bills and 5 per cent on Statutory Instruments.

The Crown

The Crown's role today is largely ceremonial but it still has an important function in approving bills so that they become acts and in the opening and dissolution of Parliaments. The government's programme of work is set out in the Queen's Speech at the beginning of each session of Parliament.

Parliamentary business and procedures

Parliamentary procedures are complex, have developed and evolved over hundreds of years and continue to change in order to adapt to changes in the world around Parliament and the demands placed upon it. The authoritative handbook for Parliamentary procedure is known in short as *Erskine May* or *Parliamentary Practice*, is published by Lexis Nexis and is in its 24th edition. However, you will now find most of the detail on the Parliamentary website.

Parliamentary sessions

The life of a Parliament is a maximum of five years and runs from the date of one general election to the next. However, in practice, around four years has been more common as it is the incumbent Prime Minister who decides when to request the Sovereign to dissolve Parliament and call a General Election, and the decision is made when it is electorally advantageous to do so. The Coalition government has proposed that there should in future be fixed-term Parliaments of five years which, if the appropriate legislation is passed, will mean the next General Election takes place on 7 May 2015.

Each Parliament is divided into sessions that usually run from the State Opening by the Monarch in November to Prorogation or the 'suspending' of Parliament the following October. The first session following a general election in the spring or summer usually lasts longer, until the November of the following year. If Parliament approves the legislation to introduce fixed-term Parliaments then each session will, starting from May 2012, commence in May each year. Parliament may be recalled during a recess in an emergency, as happened, for example, on the death of the Queen Mother following the terrorist attacks in New York and Washington in 2001 and during the civil unrest of the summer of 2011.

The usual pattern is:

- State Opening (usually November) until shortly before Christmas;

- early January until Easter (except for a recess week in February);

- Easter until late July (except for a recess week at the Spring Bank Holiday);

- early October until Prorogation.

The number of days in a session when Parliament sits will vary and over the past thirty years has been as high as 244 days during the 1979–80 session and as low as 60 during the

2009–10 session when a general election was held in May 2010. Details of the sitting times for the House of Commons, Westminster Hall and the House of Lords are on the Parliament website, and most easily found as part of an extensive set of Frequently Asked Questions (FAQs). These cover many aspects of the work of Parliament including the number of days and hours the House of Commons has sat during a Parliamentary session, the average cost of Early Day Motions and the number of divisions or votes in a Parliamentary session.

The pattern of sittings has changed over the years and the House of Commons Information Office Factsheet P4: *Sittings of the House* describes how the current situation has evolved.

All the detail and facts and figures for a Parliamentary session are provided retrospectively through the *Sessional Information Digest* (SID) which provides a summary of the activities of a Parliamentary session and is compiled from the *Weekly Information Bulletin* (WIB). It is published on the Parliament website under Publications and Records.

House of Commons

In the chamber of the Commons, the Prime Minister, Cabinet ministers, and the Leader of the Opposition and Shadow ministers sit on the front benches opposite each other. MPs who do not hold office as ministers or shadow ministers are known as 'backbenchers'. A backbencher has four roles:

- to support his party (the partisan role);
- to represent his constituency;
- to hold the government to account (the scrutiny role);
- to contribute to legislation (the legislative role).

The House of Commons sits from 2.30–10.30pm on Mondays and Tuesdays, 11.30am–7.30pm on Wednesdays,

10.30am–6.30pm on Thursdays and 9.30am–3pm on sitting Fridays. The Parliament website lists the Fridays when the house will sit during a Parliamentary session.

The order of business can be found on the Parliamentary Business page under the tab for the House of Commons and an RSS feed is available to help in keeping track of Commons business.

Westminster Hall

Westminster Hall is a separate meeting place first used in November 1999 to allow more backbench debates.

Sittings of the House take place in Westminster Hall on Tuesdays and Wednesdays from 9.30am to 11.30am and 2.00pm to 4.30pm, and on Thursdays from 2.30pm to 5.30pm. Extra time may be allowed here if there have been suspensions of the meetings owing to divisions in the House or a Committee of the Whole House.

The programme of business is available under the tab for Westminster Hall under House of Commons on the Parliamentary Business section of the UK Parliament website and there is an RSS feed covering the business to be discussed.

The proceedings of meetings held in Westminster Hall are recorded in *Hansard* as well as those of debates in the House of Commons and the House of Lords but the entry is given the suffix 'WH' to distinguish them. Future business is listed as part of the *House of Commons Future Business* webpage under section B.

House of Lords

In the House of Lords there are government, opposition and cross benches, and the bishops sit to the right of the Speaker.

The House sits on Mondays, Tuesdays and Wednesdays starting with questions to government at 2.30pm (3pm on Wednesdays), followed by legislative business and from 7.30pm a short debate, with the House aiming to rise at 10pm. On Thursdays the sitting starts at 11am with oral questions and then debates a variety of topics, rising at 7pm. On Fridays from 10am the House debates proposals for new laws from backbenchers.

The Order Paper sets out the business of the day and the programme of business is published on the website under the tab for the House of Lords on the Parliamentary Business page. The business of the House is recorded by *Hansard* reporters as in the Commons and published on the website by 8am the next day and in hard copy by 7.30am.

Details of how the Lords functions and its role and procedures can be found in the *House of Lords Guide to Business* published on the Parliament website and in *The Work of the House of Lords – Its Role, Functions and Powers* also on the Parliament website.

Parliamentary business

The role of Parliament has been described above as raising taxation, scrutinising the government, passing laws and debating various issues. To fulfil this role it has a well established pattern of business.

The daily routine of business in Parliament is set out in what is known as the Vote Bundle and in the *What's on* section of the Parliament website. The detailed set of *Business Papers* is also available under the tab for *Current Day's Business* on the *Publications and Records* section of the Parliament website.

In each House the sittings begin with prayers followed by Question Time. In the House of Commons MPs have an hour to put questions to government ministers and on Wednesdays to the Prime Minister. There is an *Order of Oral Questions* published which is a rota of which government departments will be answering questions and it appears in the *Weekly Information Bulletin* (WIB). In the House of Lords Members have just half an hour to place questions and these are addressed to the government as a whole.

Questions are followed by an opportunity for ministers to make a Ministerial Statement to the House which will be on a topical issue. For instance, Lord Adonis announced the publication of the proposed route of a high-speed rail link from London Euston to Birmingham in a Ministerial Statement to the House of Lords in March 2010. Ministers can be questioned on the statement made and the statement may be repeated in the other House.

Questions may receive written answers and Ministerial Statements may also be given in writing. These will appear in *Hansard*. A statement about future business is made on Thursdays.

After questions and ministerial statements are complete both Houses will debate legislation or matters of concern. Adjournment debates take place for half an hour at the end of each day's sitting and are an opportunity to debate a variety of issues although no vote is taken afterwords. For the Thursday debate the topic is chosen by the Speaker and for the remainder of sessions by a ballot.

Part of the business of Parliament for Members is, of course, to vote on the topics debated and this is done through Divisions. By tradition Members walk through division lobbies to indicate the way they wish to vote at the end of a debate. For more information on how these work see the House of Commons Information Office Factsheet P9: *Divisions*.

The main activities of Parliament are communicated through its website and a series of publications. Many documents are required each day to enable Parliament to function. In the House of Commons these are known collectively as the Vote Bundle and are essential tools for Members and the public to keep abreast of the business being addressed. The Vote Bundle 'consists of a set of papers including the Order Paper, some printed on white, and others on blue paper, containing information about the business of the day, the transactions of the previous day's sitting, and notices for future days'. It is available on the Parliament website.

Current business

There is a link to *Today's Business* from the home page of the Parliament website which gives details of the debates etc. for the day. You may sign up for email alerts to the *Summary Agenda* and *Order of Business*.

The Order of Business includes subjects for debate, written ministerial statements, and Oral PQs for the day, and the Summary Agenda provides an overview of the day's business. Together they make up the *Order Paper*. (The Lords has its own Order Paper known as *Notices and Orders of the Day.*) These are available in print and on the website and form part of the *Vote Bundle*.

The debates are webcast and may be viewed via the website. BBC Parliament broadcasts debates and select committee hearings and these are also brought together on the BBC Democracy Live website at: *www.bbc.co.uk/ democracylive*. You may also attend debates – for more information on this see the section on visiting Parliament at the end of this chapter.

Future business

It is useful to know about forthcoming Parliamentary business in order to monitor a particular subject, track the progress of a particular piece of legislation, or offer an alerting service to your organisation. Using these sources below will enable you to do that.

- *Parliamentary calendar (services.parliament.uk/calendar).* allows you to see the programme of business for each of the Chambers, Westminster Hall, General Committees and Select Committees. You can select to see the programme for today, this week or future business.

- *Business statement.* Every Thursday while the Commons is sitting, the Leader of the House makes a statement on the business of the House for the following week and may look further ahead in some instances. This statement is reported in *Hansard* the following day and the information also appears on the website of the Leader of the House at: *www.commonsleader.gov.uk.*

- *Weekly Information Bulletin.* The WIB takes its information from the statement of the Leader of the House but may also include business that has not yet been confirmed so it forms a source of possible future events. It may be accessed on the Parliament website where it is available from 4.00pm on Fridays and is published every week that the House is sitting. The print version is issued on a Saturday and published by TSO but may take a day or two by post. It includes the main proceedings of the Commons – forthcoming business, subjects for debate, Committee sittings and so on – and selected information from the Lords, including committee sittings. It was first published in 1978. You will find further information in the HCIO Factsheet P17: *Guide to the Weekly Information Bulletin.*

- *Forthcoming Parliamentary Questions.* Questions for Oral Answer and a list of PQs may be found in the Vote Bundle. Questions to be answered in writing that day and those that have been tabled for answer at a future date are listed respectively in Parts 1 and 2 of *Questions for Oral or Written Answer*.

Previous business

Hansard

The record of the proceedings of Parliament is held in what is normally referred to as *Hansard*. Strange as it may seem to us today, the debates of the House of Commons were originally held in secret and this secrecy was not challenged until the seventeenth century. The Official Report or *Hansard* was eventually established and the way in which a record of the proceedings of Parliament is to be made is set out in Erskine May's book *A Practical Treatise on the Law, Privileges, Proceedings and Usage of Parliament*, otherwise known as *Parliamentary Practice*, first published in 1844 and now in its 23rd edition. Erskine May states that the Official Report 'though not strictly verbatim, is substantially the verbatim report, with repetitions and redundancies omitted and with obvious mistakes corrected, but which on the other hand leaves out nothing that adds to the meaning of the speech or illustrates the argument'. Debates in the Commons Chamber and Westminster Hall are recorded in the *Commons Hansard*. There is a separate *Hansard* for the Lords. The raw transcript of a debate is usually available within 3 hours of the end of the debate on the Parliament website. After editing, which includes the addition of column numbers making it possible to cite Hansard is published on the web and in print normally by 6am the next day. Videos of previous debates and proceedings may be found in the video and audio archive on the website. These remain on the site for 12 months.

Sessional Information Digest (SID)

The Sessional Information Digest brings together information about the business of each Parliamentary session and 'acts as an index and companion to the WIB but does not wholly supersede it' (Butcher, 1991). It provides facts and figures such as the number of PQs and the number of divisions, and covers legislation, listing different types of bills, providing a subject index to white papers and green papers and details of Membership, and detailing the work of committees.

Voting records

You may check on how MPs voted on particular issues or check their voting record through *Hansard*. *Hansard* records the 'divisions' in one of two ways. It may record the division immediately after a particular debate or, now the House has introduced 'deferred divisions', it will record deferred divisions each Wednesday after the business of the day. A deferred division is when MPs complete and sign a ballot paper instead of walking through the 'Aye' or 'No' lobbies. There were just seven of these in the 2009–10 session of Parliament out of a total of 135 divisions.

The Commons Library publishes *MPs' Participation in Divisions* in the Standard Notes series. The first edition published covered the 2001–02 session. The publications show the number of Commons divisions in which each MP participated as a percentage of the divisions for the period covered and other data such as the total number of divisions and the average participation rate.

You may also check MPs' voting records on *www. theyworkforyou.com*, although, of course, this is not an official site.

Debate in Parliament

Parliamentary Questions (PQs)

PQs are a key tool for use by an MP in their scrutiny role. Oral PQs are, as the name suggests, answered orally by the

Prime Minister (PM) or a departmental minister. Prime Minister's Question Time (PMQs) takes place once a week on a Wednesday and days are scheduled for answers on a daily basis from different departments in the House. These answers appear in the appropriate place within the report of proceedings in *Hansard*. Written Parliamentary Questions (WPQs), by far the most numerous, appear in a separately paginated sequence at the end of each daily part of *Hansard* and are arranged by department and given a subject heading. Questions may be on any topic and while most replies are short they can be a valuable source of information (including extensive tables or statistics) or in a format that would be difficult, perhaps impossible, to find elsewhere.

If a large number of questions have been answered on a particular day, they may appear in a separate sequence, dated the day they were answered, in a subsequent issue of *Hansard*. PQs appear on the Parliament website and may be retrieved by a search which can be restricted to WPQs. An MP will sometimes ask a series of PQs on the same or very similar subject of a range of departments. It is sometimes interesting to compare the answers but note, however, that PQs on the same topic may be allocated slightly different subject headings. The Lords *Hansard* also contains PQs, although fewer are tabled in the Lords, and these are indexed at the end of each daily part. For more detailed information about PQs see House of Commons Information Office Factsheet P1: *Parliamentary Questions*.

Early Day Motions

Early Day Motions (EDMs) are used by MPs to highlight particular concerns, although some have recently questioned their usefulness. They are formal motions submitted for debate but very few are actually debated. They are a useful tool for MPs for 'publicising the views of individual MPs, drawing attention to specific events or campaigns, and demonstrating the extent of parliamentary support for a particular cause or point of view' (Parliament website). They have little procedural significance but may be used by the Whips to assess how much support there is for a particular subject. They include both national and local matters. EDMs are listed in the Vote Bundle (see Business of Parliament below) and there is an EDM database which covers all EDMs from the 1997–98 Session on the Parliament website. The database allows users to view information about current EDMs and then to search by name the Members who have signed them or by topics covered and by number and description. It is important to note that you need to select the session you wish to search from the top navigation bar. It is not possible to search all sessions together.

Details of EDMs from 1989 through to 1997 are available from the House of Commons Information Office. For anything earlier you will need to contact the Parliamentary Archives at: *www.parliament.uk/publications/archives.cfm.*

Examples of EDMs from 2010 include one with the title *Non-domiciled Taxpayers and Parliament* which was signed by six MPs, tabled in March 2010 and described as follows:

> That this House believes that citizens who choose to have non-domiciled status, and thus avoid paying tax on income earned outside the United Kingdom, should be debarred from being a Member of either House of Parliament.

From an earlier era an EDM under the title *Great Britain Rugby League Team Victory Over Australia* was signed by 83 MPs and described as follows:

> That this House congratulates the Great Britain Rugby League team on their magnificent 19–12 victory over

Australia on Saturday 27th October; notes that this was the first British victory over a touring Australian side since 1978 and ends the Kangaroos' 37 match unbeaten run on British soil; commends the Australian team for their contribution to a first-class sporting occasion; and wishes the Lions every success in the remaining two matches of the Ashes series.

For more detailed information about EDMs see House of Commons Information Office Factsheet P3: *Early Day Motions.*

Legislative process

Typically 20 or 30 Acts of Parliament will be enacted every year but this is the final stage of what may have been a long and complex process. The process begins with formulation of policy by the government or by the governing party with perhaps an airing at the annual party conference. It may appear in the party manifesto as a policy to be implemented if the party is elected and, if the party is in power, then it may be announced in the Queen's Speech as part of the forthcoming legislative programme. What will probably follow will be a Green Paper, a consultative document, with a closing date for comments, and after this a White Paper giving the definitive view on the subject. The next stage will be to introduce a bill in Parliament which, being a government bill, will almost certainly become an Act in due course. However, all bills are susceptible to amendment during their passage, especially in relation to their detailed provisions. A government with a reasonable majority can pretty much guarantee its legislative programme because it controls almost all Parliamentary business time.

The legislative process is very clearly set out on the Parliament website where you may view a Flash presentation which takes you through the stages. House of Commons Information Office Factsheet L1 covers the *Parliamentary Stages of a Government Bill*.

Queen's Speech

At the State Opening of Parliament, usually held in November each year, the Queen will make a speech in the House of Lords in which she will outline her government's legislative programme for the next session of Parliament. The speech will appear on the Parliament website as part of the Lords' *Hansard*, will be published as an un-numbered Command paper by TSO and will be included on the website of the Leader of the House of Commons at: *www.commonsleader.gov.uk*.

Green Paper

A Green Paper may appear in print and digital formats, or perhaps increasingly digital only, on the responsible department's website. If available in print, it may be published by TSO or by the lead department. A Green Paper proposes a way to tackle a particular issue and is a discussion or consultation document. Often, the government will publish some or all of the responses to its consultation. To find these you will need to check the relevant departmental website.

To keep track of these consultations there are now a number of tools available. Most departmental websites offer RSS feeds so that you can receive news of new consultations through an RSS reader.

The government's main website Directgov carries links to the consultation pages of many public sector bodies and *www.info4local.gov.uk* provides an email alerting service listing new and closing consultations.

White Paper

Once a consultation is complete the government may publish a White Paper setting out its policy on a topic, having taken into account the responses received to the consultation.

Draft bills

Since 1997, there has been an increase in the number of bills published as draft bills before they are formally introduced into Parliament. This allows for scrutiny and consultation ahead of the main legislative process. Details of all draft bills currently under consideration may be found on the Parliament website and there is also a link to any relevant select committee reports. Draft bills are listed from the 2002–03 session onwards. All draft bills are published as Command Papers and are available from TSO.

To keep track of these you will need to sign up to the email alerts on the *Draft Bills before Parliament* page of the Parliament website.

Bills

The majority of bills which are debated by Parliament are public bills which change the law as it applies to the general population and are most often introduced by the government. Some public bills may be introduced by Members, in which case they are known as Private Members' Bills (see below for more on these).

Generally bills may start in either House although controversial government bills are almost always introduced in the Commons. Finance bills and those concerned mainly with taxation or expenditure always start in the Commons.

A particularly useful page on the Parliament website – *Bills and Legislation* – maps the progress of current bills through each stage and has links to supporting documentation, including the text of the bill and explanatory notes. At a glance you can see the type of bill, the sponsor and the stage reached by any of the bills currently being considered by Parliament, as well as information on all the stages through which it must pass. There is a link to the latest version of the bill and any other bill documents, and a summary of the bill. You may sign up for either an RSS feed or an email alert so as to be able to keep track of the bill's progress.

The House of Commons Library produces politically impartial and factual Research Papers on new bills and they are available as a link from the web page for a bill. These are an excellent source of briefing material and will also contain a variety of opinions on the subject of the bill. They are produced before the second reading and after the committee stage in the Commons.

Other bills

The process outlined above applies to government bills but there are also Private Members' Bills, Private and Personal Bills and Hybrid Bills. These are described below.

Private Members' Bills

A Private Member's Bill is a public bill so it will affect the law as it applies to the general public but it is sponsored by a member of either House who is not a minister. For detailed information about Private Members' Bills and the procedures linked to them, see House of Commons Information Office Factsheets L2: *Private Members' Bill Procedure* and L3: *The Success of Private Members' Bills*.

Private and Personal Bills

It is possible for individuals or organisations outside the House such as local authorities or companies and in rare cases individuals to produce Private Bills 'to obtain powers for themselves in excess of, or in conflict with, the general law'. There are relatively few of these but recent examples include the Allhallows Staining Bill 2009/10 which removes certain statutory restrictions applying to land which makes up the site of the former church of Allhallows Staining, its churchyard and other adjoining land in the City of London and was promoted by the Clothworkers' Company, and the Kent County Council Filming on Highways Bill which was seeking powers for the county council to close the highway in order to allow filming to take place.

The progress of Private Bills can be tracked under *Bills and Legislation* and then *Private Bills* on the Parliament website.

Private bills are printed at the expense of the promoter and legal firms engaged in this specialist work are listed in the *Weekly Information Bulletin* (WIB). They are not considered to be Parliamentary publications. They must be accompanied by explanatory notes and they should not be confused with Private Member's Bills (see above).

For further information see House of Commons Information Office Factsheet L4: *Private Bills*.

Hybrid Bills

There is one further type of bill and that is a combination of a public and private bill and is basically one which affects the nation but also specific groups or individuals. Examples are bills such as those which introduced rail lines, an example being the Channel Tunnel bills, and the one that will be required for the high-speed rail link between London Euston and Birmingham and beyond. See House of Commons Information Office Factsheet L5: *Hybrid Bills* for more information.

Progress of a bill

House of Commons

A bill now normally has six stages in its journey through the House of Commons. These will be:

- First Reading
- Public Reading Stage
- Second Reading
- Committee Stage (consideration by committee)
- Report Stage (consideration by the House on report from committee) and
- Third Reading.

First Reading

A bill is first announced in the Order Paper, and on that day the Clerk reads the short title of the bill and a notional day for the Second Reading is named. Usually the first and second reading stages are separated by at least two weekends but it is not invariably so. A bill is given a bill number on the day that its short title is read and this is printed in the bottom left-hand corner of the front page of the printed version. It is important to remember that every time the bill is reprinted, for example to take account of amendments after the

Committee stage or when a bill moves between the Houses, it is given a new number. However, the Lords publish amendments to its public bills within the bill series. These retain the same number as the original bill but with a suffix of lower-case letters or roman numerals.

Public Reading Stage

The Coalition government committed to introducing a public reading stage in its *Programme for Government* published in June 2010 and it was first used for the Protection of Freedoms Bill in February 2011. The Public Reading Stage allows time within the process for members of the public to comment on the content of the bill and this is done through a website. Comments can be made from the time the bill is first introduced into the House until it is first debated. As the convention is that there should be two weekends between the time the bill is introduced and is first debated, the period for comment by the public will be about two weeks. Comments are then 'digested' by the sponsoring department and forwarded to MPs.

Second Reading

Second Reading is when the House considers the principle of the bill, often in lengthy debate, and this will be recorded in *Hansard*. The date for the Second Reading is announced in Thursday's *Business Statement* and will also appear in the 'Forthcoming Business' section of the *Weekly Information Bulletin* (WIB).

Committee Stage

The Committee Stage is the point at which the bill is examined in detail. There are four types of committee but the two most common are the *Public Bill Committee* which is a sub-set of the General Committees and a *Committee of the Whole House* where the bill is taken on the floor of the House. A

Public Bill Committee (prior to Session 2006–07 they were called Standing Committees) is created anew for each bill. The Committee consists of about 16 members, reflecting the party composition of the House but including a minister from the sponsoring department and front-bench opposition spokespersons.

The committee will (if it is allowed parliamentary time – by no means always the case), examine the bill line by line, each clause and schedule, and may also consider amendments and, indeed, new clauses and schedules. The proceedings of a Committee of the Whole House appear with the normal record of the House in *Hansard*. Proceedings of Committees appear on the *Committee* section of the website as part of the record of the progress of a bill. Printed copies are published separately by TSO in single parts for each sitting, followed by a softbound collection of all the daily parts. A consolidated (case bound) volume for each bill is published after consideration is complete. Public Bill Committee proceedings still form a part of *Hansard* but the publication timetable for the *Committee Hansard* is different from the main *Hansard*. The aim is to secure print publication within two working days.

Amendments to bills in committee may be found in the Vote Bundle under 'Lists of Amendments'. Amendments tabled the previous day are printed on blue paper to show that they are new and not for the current day's business. However, for its first meeting, the committee will have a 'Marshalled list' on white paper of all amendments up to those tabled the previous day. Amendments are numbered but do not necessarily appear in numerical order as they are arranged according to the part of the bill to which they apply.

Standing Committee Debates (SCDeb) came to prominence following the *Pepper v. Hart* decision in the Lords in 1992 which allowed *Hansard,* of which they form an integral part, to be referred to in the interpretation of the intentions of an

Act of Parliament when the wording of an Act is 'ambiguous or obscure'. Previously this was felt to go against the principle of freedom of speech and Article 9 of the 1689 Bill of Rights. It is now felt that the addition of explanatory notes to Acts of Parliament make it less likely that the courts will need to resort to this source of information when interpreting the law.

Uncompleted bills always used to fall at Prorogation but there are now arrangements for bills to be carried over from one session to the next. The first such example was the Financial Services and Markets Bill (session 1998–99). When a bill is carried over it may be allocated to a general committee with a different letter than the one in the previous session. This may cause confusion as, for instance, up to clause 50 it may be allocated to Committee B, but having been carried forward to the next session, clause 51 onwards may be allocated to Committee D.

Report Stage and Third Reading

After the bill has been debated in Committee stage, the Committee will report the bill with amendments to the Chamber for further debate before the whole House. This is known as the Report Stage and is followed by the Third Reading. For the Third Reading the debate is usually short and amendments cannot be made. When it is complete the House will vote to approve the bill. These latter two stages appear in *Hansard*.

House of Lords

When the bill has completed its progress through the Commons it is then sent to the Lords where it will go through a process broadly similar to that of the Commons. (If the Bill was originally introduced into the Lords it will pass to the Commons.) The principal differences from the point of view of publication is that many bills are taken on the floor of the House and debates therefore appear in *Hansard* for the Lords and amendments may be moved on Third Reading.

Moving between Chambers

Bills may move between Houses several times if Members disagree. If certain criteria are met, eventually the bill can be passed without the consent of the Lords but not until the next session of Parliament. This situation arose with the Hunting Bill in 2004 and the legislation which allows this to happen is in the Parliament Bill 1911 as amended by the Parliament Act 1949.

Royal Assent

When these criteria have been met or when the text has been agreed by both Houses, the bill receives Royal Assent. Today this is usually announced to the Commons and the Lords and recorded in *Hansard*. Royal Assent has not been refused since 1707 and has not been given in person since 1854. After Royal Assent the bill becomes an Act and is published by TSO on behalf of the Queen's Printer. The Act of Parliament is then also published on the Official Legislation website (*www.legislation.gov.uk*) and will in due course be added to the Revised Legislation (formerly Statute Law) Database which is also available via the Legislation website.

Acts or sections of acts do not necessarily come into effect immediately or, occasionally, at all. An example of an Act which has not come into force is the 1928 Easter Act which was to fix the date of Easter as the 'first Sunday after the second Saturday in April'. The Act remains on the Statute Book and requires Parliament to give regard to 'any opinion officially expressed by any Church or other Christian body'.

As no willingness to make the change has yet been expressed, this Act remains in place but not active.

Secondary or delegated legislation

There are a number of other types of legislation beyond Acts of Parliament. The procedures that surround their development can be complex and it is best to use the House of Commons Information Office Factsheets and the Parliament website generally to look at specific measures such as Hybrid Instruments and Legislative Reform Orders etc. However, one type of secondary legislation you are very likely to come across and to need to find is a Statutory Instrument.

Statutory Instruments

Statutory Instruments are the most common form of secondary legislation and are often the detailed regulations and orders needed to bring an Act of Parliament into force. They may also be used to make changes to the requirements of an Act but this will have to be within the powers set out in the original legislation. In 2009 there were 3,499 Statutory Instruments published compared with fewer than 30 acts, and this would be a typical year. An Act of Parliament may well set out what is required in quite general terms but will rely on Statutory Instruments to give the detailed and practical regulations and orders which are needed so that the Act can be brought into force. They are made by or under powers conferred by or under statute on Her Majesty in Council or on a Minister, the Welsh Ministers or other body or person. Since June 2004 all instruments required to be laid before Parliament have been accompanied by an Explanatory Memorandum 'setting out a brief statement of the purpose of an instrument and providing information about its policy objective and policy implications'. All Statutory Instruments are available on the Legislation website back to 1987, listed by date and number and as html files or as pdfs, and with an Explanatory Memorandum where produced.

Finding an SI using the search on the new Legislation website is a relatively easy task if you know the title or part of it and the year it was issued, though this may result in a large number of results. There is an advanced search which allows you to limit your search by keyword, date, type of legislation, area and date range which can help to restrict the number of results returned. If you know the year and number then finding an SI is very quick and easy.

They are essential tools for ensuring the requirements of legislation are set out in practical terms and making adjustments and changes to the detail of legislation within the requirements of the original act. To use an example relevant to this book, the Freedom of Information Act 2000 was supported by the Freedom of Information Act 2000 (Commencement No. 4) Order 2004 (SI 2004/1909) which set out how and when the Act was to come into force and the Freedom of Information and Data Protection (Appropriate Limit and Fees) Regulations 2004 (SI 2004/3244) which sets out when and how much public authorities can charge for responding to requests for information. The Act was then extended to cover additional public authorities through the Freedom of Information (Additional Public Authorities) Order 2008 (SI 2008 No. 1271).

As with all legislation, most Statutory Instruments are subject to scrutiny within the Parliamentary processes but the procedures vary depending on the requirements of the Act to which they relate. Details may be found in the House of Commons Information Office Factsheet L7: Statutory Instruments.

Church Measures/Instruments

Church Measures/Instruments are changes to ecclesiastical law and are developed by the General Synod of the Church of England, the ruling body of the Church, and presented to the Ecclesiastical Committee of Parliament for consideration. Both Houses must approve the Measure before it is presented for Royal Assent. For details see House of Commons Information Office Factsheet L10: *Church of England Measures.*

Special Procedure Orders

Special Procedure Orders 'are a form of delegated legislation to which special parliamentary procedure applies. An example might be a Compulsory Purchase Order of land for road building. Part of this procedure gives those people or bodies who are especially affected by the order (the right) to petition against it to either House. If successful, such petitions are heard by a Joint Committee consisting of Members from both Houses' (Parliament website).

Explanatory notes and further information

Since 1999 most Public Acts have been published with explanatory notes which are designed to help people understand the meaning and implications of the Act. Statutory Instruments have been accompanied by explanatory memoranda since 2004 and Finance Acts since 2009.

Accessing enacted legislation

The *legislation.gov.uk* website is the official source for UK-based legislation once it has been enacted, containing both the original version as it was enacted and the revised texts from what was known as the Statute Law Database.

When new legislation is produced it will almost inevitably affect existing legislation, and legislation therefore has to be consolidated to show the changes made to existing legislation.

The website is managed by the National Archives which, with the Office of the Queen's Printer for Scotland, is responsible for publication in hard copy and on the web of:

- Public General Acts (PGA)

- Local Acts

- Acts of the Scottish Parliament

- Acts of the Northern Ireland Assembly

- Measures of the National Assembly for Wales.

The text is initially available as originally enacted with no information about subsequent revisions or amendments through later legislation.

The website provides access to the full text as enacted of:

- UK Parliament Public General Acts from 1988 onwards;

- pdfs of original versions of legislation which remains in force back to 1801.

All pre-1988 legislation is available as full text in print versions from The Stationery Office (*www.tso.co.uk*).

Chronological Tables of Local Acts from 1797 to 2007 and Personal and Private Acts from 1539–2006 were first prepared as a result of a decision by the Statute Law Commission and can be a useful tool for tracing legislation if the date of an Act is known.

To keep informed of new legislation, use the RSS feeds on the Parliament website where you can select an individual bill and sign up for the RSS feed or email updates so that you can monitor its progress throughout the process. Alternatively if you are only interested to know when an Act has received

Royal Assent, use the Legislation website and the link to *New Legislation* where you can see all legislation published in the preceding two weeks and sign up for RSS feeds for

- all legislation
- UK Acts
- UK Statutory Instruments
- Acts of the Northern Ireland Assembly
- Northern Ireland Orders in Council
- Northern Ireland Statutory Rules
- Acts of the Scottish Parliament
- Scottish Statutory Instruments
- Measures of the National Assembly for Wales.

Revised statutes

New legislation will almost always have an impact on existing legislation either by altering it, adding to it or repealing all or part of it. Being able to access the text of an Act or Statutory Instrument as originally passed is not, therefore, sufficient and some way of seeing what changes have been made subsequently by other legislation is essential. An online statute book which would provide this free of charge over the web was first proposed in the early 1990s but it took until 2006 for it to become a reality.

The Statute Law Database (SLD) was developed by the Statutory Publications Offices in London and Belfast and it is 'the primary legislation of a public general nature in force at a particular time'. Until 1991 a loose-leaf publication *Statutes in Force* (SIF) had provided a consolidated version of the law. When that ceased to be published there was nothing except expensive subscription services from companies such as Lexis Nexis or Westlaw to provide this information. SIF was used as the baseline for the SLD and it in turn had been derived mainly from *Statutes of the Realm* published from 1810 to 1828 and containing the full text of public Acts of Parliament enacted up to 1713.

In 2009 responsibility for the SLD passed to the National Archives and work continues to bring it up to date. The Statute Law Database forms the basis of the revised legislation which is now available on the *legislation.gov.uk* website. All legislation up to 2002 has been updated with the effects of new legislation, with work continuing to update the remainder.

When looking at an item of revised legislation a message appears at the top of the Table of Contents. This will either say that there are no known outstanding changes to the Act you are viewing or that there are some changes yet to be applied. If there are outstanding changes and effects still to be applied these will be listed and the Editorial Team now aim to add changes and effects as soon as possible after legislation is passed.

For a detailed analysis of the database when it was first made publicly available see 'UK Statute Law Database: First Impressions' (*Refer*, 2007).

Select Committee system

Introduction

A key element of the process of scrutinising the work of the government is through the select committee system. Select committees examine the work of specific government departments and agencies.

Departmental select committees

The present arrangements for departmental select committees began in 1979 when a committee was set up to monitor each major Whitehall department. The committees' remits evolve as Whitehall evolves. For example, in 2009 the Department for Business and Skills was formed from the Department for Business, Enterprise and Regulatory Reform and the Department for Innovation, Universities and Skills. As a result the Committee for Business, Innovation and Skills was created replacing the Business and Enterprise Committee and the Trade and Industry Committee. The Parliament website carries details of the select committees, their remit and something of their lineage, and the House of Commons Information Office has published a factsheet on *Departmental Select Committees* (Factsheet P2) which gives a more detailed description.

There are 19 departmental select committees. Most have between 11 and 14 members, proportionate to party representation in the House. Most, but not all, committees are chaired by a backbencher from the party in power. Committees are free to choose subjects for investigation and the public may attend most committee hearings. Each committee has a clerk, perhaps a second clerk and a small secretariat. Most have a pool of part-time advisors – experts in their fields – who offer guidance on particular inquiries. These may assist in suggesting who should be called to give evidence or possible lines of questioning to be pursued.

Note: A select committee is not to be confused with what used to be called a standing committee. Standing committees are now known as general committees and they are set up anew to examine each bill that passes through Parliament. These are covered in the section on the legislative process above.

Select committees have a remit, powers and, members, hold inquiries and issue publications. All select committees have pages on the Parliament website and can be reached by clicking on the 'Committees' link on the home page.

- *Remit (Orders of Reference)*. This will appear on the committee's website.

- *Powers*. Select committee powers stem from Parliament itself and are set out in standing orders (*www.publications. Parliament.uk/pa/cm/cmpubns*). Powers vary slightly between committees.

- *Membership*. Membership is given on the website which is the most up-to-date publicly available source as well as in commercial publications such as those Published by Vachers Dods. Membership changes are flagged up in the Order Paper but do not take effect until they have been agreed formally by the House and recorded in *Hansard*.

- *Inquiries*. All select committees hold inquiries that may be anything from a single evidence session to a lengthy and detailed inquiry from a wide range of witnesses and producing a substantial report as a conclusion. Recent examples include the Public Administration Select Committee inquiry into the concept of the Big Society, the Home Affairs Select Committee inquiry into phone hacking by the *News of the World* and the Treasury Select Committee inquiry into Competition and Choice in the Banking Sector. The terms of its current inquiry or inquiries together with a 'call for evidence' may appear on the home page of its website. A committee may issue a press release announcing a new inquiry. The 'call for evidence' states the subject of the inquiry and requests written evidence by a specified date.

- *Publications*. Select committees publish in both print and digital forms. Indeed, select committee publications form part of the House of Commons papers series published by TSO. Committees publish the full text of their 'Minutes of Evidence' and 'Reports' on their websites and some go back to the 1997–98 session. Westminster Hall provides a fortnightly slot on Thursday afternoons for select committee reports to be debated.

- *Hearings.* The website gives details of the date, time, venue and witnesses attending forthcoming hearings. Most are held at Westminster but committees sometimes travel both in the UK and abroad. Hearings are listed in the WIB but the best source is a committee's web page which gives details of forthcoming hearings and inquiries. Email alerts, to which you may subscribe, give details of forthcoming hearings.

The House of Commons (and the Lords) Information Office will also supply details of hearings. For information on very recent high-profile hearings some newspapers' coverage may be available and you may watch a webcast of the hearing live or from the archive through the Parliament website. Committees now put 'uncorrected transcripts' of evidence from many hearings on their web pages within 24–48 hours of the hearing. The *Parliamentary Calendar* on the website lists forthcoming public meetings and the dates of debates on committee reports in Westminster Hall. Uncorrected evidence is the transcript of evidence that witnesses (and the committee) have not yet corrected and is the format in which most evidence will appear. It is important to be aware of this as occasionally the text may be misleading.

For the text of past investigations not available digitally, you may trace them through TSO (*www.tso.co.uk*) and through the HMSO/TSO annual catalogues. Texts may be obtained from a suitable library or, in many cases, from TSO's 'print on demand' service.

Select committees now produce annual reports (instead of the previous informal unpublished notes), published as House of Commons Papers and numbered within the sequence of ordinary reports. These are a useful record of committees' activities and are available from TSO and on the Parliament website.

The government should deliver its response to all select committee reports within two months. These will either be published by the committee within the House of Commons Paper series and numbered within the sequence of ordinary reports, or by the government. If published by the government then they will be published as a Command Paper and are available from TSO and via the Official Documents site (*www.official-documents.gov.uk*) but not with the committee publications.

(This site contains a complete collection of Command Papers and House of Commons Papers produced by government departments from 17 May 2005 to the present. It also has some Command Papers back to 2004, House of Commons Papers from the 2002–03 session to the present and other papers from 2005 to date.)

Lords select committees

The Lords has its own select committee system and publishes a weekly printed guide to committee hearings, *House of Lords Committees Weekly Bulletin*. Lords select committees include the Economic Affairs, Delegated Powers and Regulatory Reform and EU committees. Lords select committees publish written, uncorrected and corrected evidence on the web.

Note that if you click on the standard *Reports and Publications* link on the left-hand side of a committee's web page, you will only find reports and corrected oral and written evidence. If you are looking for more recent (and therefore uncorrected) evidence, you need to click on the links that are on the committee's home page, below the introductory text. Committees have slightly different layouts to their web pages which may mislead you when searching for uncorrected evidence.

General committees

The proceedings of general committees (previously known as standing committees) are published daily.

Public bill committees are the general committees that examine new bills and have been described as part of the legislative process above. There are other general committees, such as the Delegated Legislation Committees for statutory instruments, also described above and Second Reading Committees. There are also the Welsh or Northern Ireland Grand Committees.

Regional select committees

Regional committees were created in 2008 and followed the appointment of regional ministers but were abolished following the 2010 General Election and the formation of the Coalition government. The Former Select Committee section of the Parliament website provides links to the information for each of the nine regional select committees, giving access to the minutes of meetings, reports and publications, press notices, the chair and contact details.

Other committees

There are other committees with specific roles within Parliament and these include, for example, the Ecclesiastical Committee which provides a link with the General Synod and the Members' Estimate Committee which is concerned with MPs' pay and allowances. As with other committees the information about their remit and publications is on the *Committee* section of the Parliament website.

The Public Accounts Committee is a high–profile committee often in the news. Its remit is to focus on value for money of the funding granted to Parliament to meet public expenditure. It looks at 'economy, effectiveness and efficiency' in areas such as the points-based system for managing immigration and the way HMRC (Her Majesty's Revenue Customs) collects taxes.

There are also Joint Committees (joint committees of both houses) which are formed from time to time perhaps to examine particular legislation.

European Parliament and Westminster

Much of the legislation developed and debated by the Houses of Parliament at Westminster emanates from Europe. Exactly how much is not known, but in a response to a Parliamentary question in the Lords in April 2009 the following statement was made:

> It has been estimated that around half of all UK legislation with an impact on business, charities and the voluntary sector stems from legislation agreed by Ministers in Brussels, but this is a category of legislation which is more likely than legislation in general to have originated in the EU. It is likely that the overall proportion is therefore much lower.
>
> (*Hansard*, 28 April 2009, col. WA28)

As one of the 27 Member States of the European Union, the UK Parliament, on behalf of the UK, attempts to monitor and scrutinise the vast amount of information and legislation which comes from the EU. For a background to EU institutions generally, see the EU website at *http://europa.eu*, and for easy-to-follow descriptions see *www.direct.gov.uk* and search for Europe. Alternatively see *www.fco.gov.uk* where the Foreign and Commonwealth Office provides *Britain in the European Union*. To quote from the Parliament website the role of Parliament in Europe is:

- to scrutinise EU draft legislation and other EU documents;
- to change UK law to reflect agreed EU legislation and treaties;
- to hold the government to account on its EU policies and negotiating positions in the EU institutions.

In practice this works by the UK Parliament receiving copies of EU documents and these are considered by the scrutiny committees in the Commons and the Lords. It should be understood that 'The EU has the authority to apply legislation in the UK but actually putting it into action may require Parliament to pass new or amended legislation' (Parliament website).

So far as legislation is concerned, it may issue from the Council of the European Union in the form of regulations, directives and decisions:

- *Regulations*. These are general in application and binding in their entirety, and directly applicable in all Member States so they do not have to be incorporated into national law. There is just one version for all Member States although it will be published in the different languages of the Union.
- *Directives*. These are binding as to the objective to be achieved by Member States but each country may decide how best to implement them in national law.
- *Decisions*. These are binding in their entirety on those to whom they are addressed.

Westminster, of course, cannot hold EU institutions to account save through UK Government representatives and Ministers attending specialist meetings of Council to consider particular legislation, for instance transport legislation. The process is complex and is conveniently and cogently explained in Commons Factsheet L11: *EU Legislation and Scrutiny Procedures*. It includes a brief account of the development of Parliamentary scrutiny since 1973.

Essentially, the system is as follows.

House of Commons

The European Scrutiny Committee considers about 1,100 EU documents per year, reports its opinion on the legal and political significance of each document and recommends further action to the House. With the majority, no further action is taken. For others, the Committee can report issues arising from a document, or refer a document to one of three European Standing Committees, or recommend that a document be debated on the Floor of the House. The European Scrutiny Committee has pages on the Parliament site which include a weekly progress report on documents and an archive of committee reports (*www.parliament.uk/escom*). The work of UK Ministers in the EU Council of Ministers is monitored by the European Scrutiny Committee through Parliamentary questions and by taking evidence from Ministers in person.

The European Standing Committees – of which there are three, each consisting of 13 MPs – take on different subject responsibilities, divided according to the work of Whitehall departments:

A – Environment, Food and Rural Affairs, Transport, Local Government and the Regions, Forestry Commission, together with those responsibilities pertaining to the Scotland, Wales, and Northern Ireland Offices.

B – HM Treasury, HM Revenue and Customs, Work and Pensions, Foreign and Commonwealth Office, International Development, Home Office, Constitutional Affairs, and other subjects not covered by the other committees.

C – Trade and Industry, Education and Skills, Culture, Media and Sport, Health.

Debates on the Floor of the House are few in number and take place only if the government is prepared to allocate time for a debate. However, a document may also be 'tagged' by the European Scrutiny Committee.

This means that while a document may not warrant a debate in its own right, it may be recommended as relevant to a debate already scheduled to take place in the House or in a European Standing Committee. This is described as being 'tagged' to that debate. A list of the European Union documents being considered by the House of Commons forms part of the Vote Bundle and can be viewed on the Parliament website. Follow the links from the home page under *Parliamentary Business* to *Business Papers*.

House of Lords

The Lord's European Union Select Committee produces reports on fewer documents than the Commons committee but, via its sub-committees, conducts detailed inquiries on particular policy areas. The sub-committees are:

- Sub-Committee A: Economic and Financial Affairs and International Trade
- Sub-Committee B: Internal Market
- Sub-Committee C: Foreign Affairs, Defence and Development Policy
- Sub-Committee D: Environment and Agriculture

- Sub-Committee E: Law and Institutions
- Sub-Committee F: Home Affairs
- Sub-Committee G: Social Policy and Consumer Affairs.

As well as scrutinising European documents by taking reports from these sub-committees, the Lord's European Select Committee will take evidence from the Minister for Europe after each European Council, scrutinises the work programme of the Commission and generally takes a strategic overview of EU issues. To keep abreast of their discussions use their monthly newsletter published on the Parliament website and found by following the links to *Committees* and then *Lords Select Committees* and 'EU – Select Committee' (subscribe by emailing *euclords@parliament.uk*). They also publish an annual report.

The Commons and Lords committees cooperate closely on EU matters.

Visiting Parliament

Tours

Parliament is open to visitors although understandably security measures are in place. Tours need to be arranged through your MP or a peer and are very popular so may need to be booked well in advance. During the summer opening, visitors, including overseas visitors, may pay for a tour either in advance or by queuing.

Debates

The public galleries of the Houses and Westminster Hall are open to UK residents and overseas visitors to watch debates.

However, free tickets are needed for Prime Minister's Question Time and are only issued to UK residents through your MP or a peer. Anyone without a ticket can queue and will be able to gain access if there is space after the ticket-holders have been accommodated. For other debates there is a public queue for everyone and it can take a couple of hours of queuing to gain access.

Committees

Attendance at public committees is open to everyone and there are meetings from Monday to Thursday when Parliament is in session. Details of the dates, times and the location of the committee room are available from the Commons Committee Calendar found by following links from the *What's on* tab on the home page of the Parliament website. It is worth checking times and venues of committee hearings as these may change, and remember to leave plenty of time to get through security.

Virtual tour

If you are unable to visit Parliament in person you can take advantage of the virtual tour of many parts including the Chambers, Lobby, Libraries and Portcullis House. Go to *www.parliament.uk/visiting* and select 'Online tours'.

Key Parliamentary information resources

Parliament website: www.parliament.uk

The main resource for accessing Parliamentary information today is, of course, *www.parliament.uk* where you will find a wealth of information about every aspect of Parliament's work from the detail of *Hansard* and Parliamentary procedure and business through to overviews of its functions and history and latest news. The search engine is being improved and results are reasonable, and there is an advanced search facility which allows selection of categories and limits by speaker and date etc. Within this site there is access to some substantial databases of information such as *Hansard*, the database of EDMs and the database of MPs.

Hansard

The *Official Report* is popularly known as *Hansard*, and while not a verbatim account, it records almost every word spoken in both Houses. It now has four sequences of pagination:

- Chamber proceedings (in ordinary type);
- Westminster Hall proceedings, including any PQs not reached (suffixed 'WH');
- Written PQ answers (in italic type);
- Written Statements (suffixed 'WS').

The information is set out in columns and the date and column number are used to reference the content of *Hansard*.

Hansard is published daily providing the record of the previous day's proceedings and is available on the web from 8am the next working day.

Same-day access to speeches in the Chamber and Westminster Hall is also available on a rolling basis on the Parliament website, with a Member's speech available within three to four hours. *Hansard* is still available in print in daily parts with a weekly cumulation and bound annual volumes. An index is produced weekly for the Lords and every two weeks for the Commons. Individual contributions in the form of speeches or interventions from MPs and peers may be retrieved by a search on the website.

The print version of the Commons *Hansard* has a separately published fortnightly index (the daily and weekly parts are un-indexed) that is also included in the bound volumes. It should be noted that references in the index are to columns, not pages. They are sometimes not entirely accurate and if you fail to find your subject in a given column it is worth scanning the columns around it. It should also be noted that it is the subject of the debate that is indexed, not issues that arise during the debate. A bound cumulative index is published at the end of the Parliamentary session.

Full records of debates are available since 1909 and before that only abbreviated versions of speeches were produced. *Hansard* has been published on the Parliament website for the House of Commons since the 1988–89 session and for the House of Lords since the 1994–95 session, and has now been digitised back to 1803.

Command Papers

Command Papers take their name from the fact that they are presented to Parliament by government Ministers 'by Command of Her Majesty' and it could be argued that they should be included in Chapter 5 on central government departments. However, although many of them are the output of government departments they are included here simply because they are 'laid before Parliament'. They are numbered consecutively with a prefix which is Cm at the moment. The numbering does not identify the Parliamentary Session and the prefix only changes when the number published with a particular prefix is close to 10,000:

- 1833–1869 1–4222
- 1870–1899 C 1–C.9550
- 1900–1918 Cd 1–Cd.9239
- 1919–1956 Cmd 1–Cmd.9889
- 1956–1986 Cmnd 1–Cmnd.9927
- 1986–   Cm 1

Some of the publications in this series are known as 'White Papers' or 'Green Papers'. White Papers are statements of government policy while Green Papers are consultative in nature and designed to open up debate on a topic. An example of a White Paper is *Digital Britain: Final Report* published in June 2009 which set out the government strategy for ensuring Britain is fit for the future in terms of broadband access and the move from analogue to digital technology. The role of Green Papers and White Papers in the legislative process is covered earlier in this chapter.

The Command Papers series also includes the following.

- Treaty Command Papers, e.g. *The Treaty of Lisbon amending the Treaty establishing the European Union and the Treaty establishing the European Community, including the protocols and annexes, and final act with declarations: Lisbon, 13 December 2007*, Cm 7294.

Treaties are published by the Foreign and Commonwealth Office (FCO) as Command Papers with Explanatory Memoranda. They are listed on the FCO website (*www.fco. gov.uk*) in order of their date of publication and alphabetically by subject back to 1997.

The Treaties Series preceded the Treaty Command Papers and these are also available on the FCO website through the database known as UK Treaties Online. It covers Command

Papers published in the Treaty Series from 1892 to 1996 inclusive.

The FCO operates a Treaty Enquiry Service (which is free of charge) open from 0900 to 1700 Monday to Friday:

Tel: 020 7008 1109.
Fax: 020 7008 1115.
Email: *treaty.fco@gtnet.gov.uk*

Written inquiries can also be made to:

Treaty Enquiry Service
Legal Advisers Directorate
Rm WLG 167
Foreign & Commonwealth Office
London
SW1A 2AH

■ Government responses to Select Committee Reports, e.g. *The Government Response to the Health Select Committee Report on Workforce Planning, Presented to Parliament by the Secretary of State for Health by Command of Her Majesty, May 2007, Cm 7085.*

The government may reply to a report from a Select Committee by the responsible Minister writing to the Committee Chairman. In these cases the response will be published by the Committee as a House of Commons Paper.

■ Reports of Committees of Inquiry, e.g. *The Stephen Lawrence Inquiry.*

Report of an Inquiry by Sir William MacPherson of Cluny advised by Tom Cook, the Right Reverend Dr John Sentamu, Dr Richard Stone. Presented to Parliament by the Secretary of State for the Home Department by Command of Her Majesty, February 1999, Cm 4262.

- Departmental and other Annual Reports e.g. *The Home Office 2009 Departmental Report*, Cm 7592.

The publication of annual reports has never been consistent, with some published as Command Papers, others as House of Commons Papers and others as departmental publications. Since June 2010 the Treasury has required departments to publish core financial and performance tables and annual reports are no longer required.

Government departments sometimes fail to publish material in the Command Paper series by mistake. This can make it more difficult to track down the required document although they are now more likely to make it available on their website.

House of Commons Information Office Factsheets

The Factsheets published by the House of Commons Information Office have been referred to frequently in the earlier sections of this chapter and are an invaluable source of information about the way Parliament functions. They are divided into four series:

- Procedure
- Legislation
- Members/Elections
- General

They are freely available on the Parliament website *www. parliament.uk/about/how/guides/factsheets1* or from the House of Commons Information Office.

> House of Commons Information Office (HCIO)
> House of Commons
> London SW1A 2TT
> Tel: 020 7219 4272

Fax: 020 7219 5839

Email: *hcinfo@Parliament.uk*

House of Commons Library publications

The House of Commons Library publishes factual and politically neutral *Research Papers* on topics of interest to MPs and their staff. These are available on the Parliament website at *www.parliament.uk/business/publications/research/research-papers*.

The Library also produces *Standard Notes* which are topical briefings prepared for MPs and particularly useful to a wider audience.

This information is available from the *Topical Issues* section on the Parliament website.

Although these documents are made available to the public, the House of Commons Library cannot provide an information service to the public and requests for information should be directed to the House of Commons Information Office.

House of Lords Information Office publications

The House of Lords Information Office publishes *The Work of the House of Lords* each year using examples from the previous Parliamentary session to explain how the House functions. It also publishes briefing papers on:

■ The work, role and function of the Lords

■ Legislation

■ Committees

■ History and Reform

and a Guide to Business.

Copies of these publications are available on the website or from:

House of Lords Information Office
House of Lords,
London SW1A 0PW
Tel: 020 7219 3107
Fax: 020 7219 0620
Email: *hlinfo@Parliament.uk*

The House of Lords Library's Library Notes

The House of Lords Library's Research Section publishes a series of Library Notes aimed at Members of Parliament and their personal staff on topical Parliamentary issues. They are available at: *www.parliament.uk/business/publications/ research/lords-library* and cover areas such as Lords ceremonial, allowances and expenses and Lords reform.

Archives

A catalogue of the Parliamentary Archive known as *Portcullis* may be found at *www.portcullis.parliament.uk* and gives details of the holdings of the Parliamentary Archive which goes back in some cases to 1497. However, the webpage carries the warning that 'apart from the printed and manuscript Journals, all the records of the House of Commons before 1834 were destroyed in the fire of that year which burnt down the old Houses of Parliament'. This is simply a catalogue of material held and photocopies will be supplied on payment of a fee.

However, we have become increasingly used to being able to access the digitised full text of material on the web and there has been substantial progress in making historic

Parliamentary material available electronically. Some digitising has been done by Parliament and some by other organisations. The Parliament website carries the following list of items which can be accessed electronically and gives details of the dates:

- Public Acts of Parliament
- Local and Private Acts of Parliament
- UK Statutory Instruments
- Parliamentary Debates – House of Commons
- Parliamentary Debates – House of Lords
- Parliamentary Papers – House of Commons
- Parliamentary Papers – House of Lords
- Deposited Papers – House of Commons and House of Lords
- Proceedings and Journals
- House of Lords Judgments
- Northern Ireland devolved Parliament and Assembly
- Parliaments of Scotland
- Welsh Assembly
- Oireachtas (Republic of Ireland).

For each of these the web page provides a link to where the information is held and a description of exactly what is included, i.e. the dates and any gaps in the content.

As this work continues, the digital access will develop and improve and users should go to *www.parliament.uk/business/ publications/parliamentary-archives/archives-electronic/* for the latest state of play.

House of Commons Parliamentary Papers (HCPP) is a subscription service and provides access to what was the Chadwyck-Healey microfiche of nineteenth- and twentieth-century House of Commons Sessional Papers. They have added the Eighteenth Century Parliamentary Papers Collection from the British Official Publications Collaborative Information Service (BOPCRIS) which covers the period 1688–1834. The University of Southampton, holders of the Ford Collection of British Official Parliamentary Publications which covers the period from 1688 to 1995, hosted BOPCRIS and with funding from the Joint Information Systems Committee (JISC) and support from the British Library digitised 39,000 eighteenth-century documents.

British History Online (*www.british-history.ac.uk*) has a section on Parliamentary Publications and provides access to publications such as the House of Commons Journal from 1547 to 1699 and the Statutes of the Realm from 1628 to 1701, as well as a variety of other resources such as the diaries of Thomas Burton MP for Westmoreland a Parliamentary diarist.

Parliamentary publications series

Most but not all of the publications of Parliament have been covered above in the most appropriate place.

For completeness a list of the series published is provided here:

- Parliamentary Business
- Weekly Information Bulletin
- Sessional Information Digest
- Votes and Proceedings (HC)
- Minutes of Proceedings (HL)
- Journals (HC and HL)
- Records of debate
- Parliamentary debates (*Hansard*) (HC and HL)
- Standing Committee debates (HC) [until session 2006–07]

- General Committee debates (HC) [from session 2006–07].
- Parliamentary papers
- House of Commons Session Papers including:
  - House of Commons bills
  - House of Commons papers.
- Command Papers
- House of Lords Sessional Papers:
  - House of Lords bills
  - House of Lords papers.
- Acts of Parliament
- Public General Acts
- Local and Personal Acts.

(Adapted from Butcher, p.22)

BBC Democracy Live

(*news.bbc.co.uk/democracylive/hi/default.stm*)

The BBC has brought together, on one website, coverage of the House of Commons, the House of Lords, Select Committees, Westminster Hall, the Scottish Parliament, the Northern Ireland Assembly, the Welsh Assembly and the European Parliament. You can use this site to watch debates in any of the above and you can register to follow the contribution made by a member or representative at any of these bodies.

Other resources

There are a number of sources of information which are not strictly within our definition of 'official' but are very useful and should not be overlooked.

TheyWorkForYou.com (*www.theyworkforyou.com*)

A website run by mysociety, a registered charity, TheyWorkForYou offers extensive information on MPs, including their voting record. It also covers Peers, Members of the Scottish Parliament and Members of the Legislative Assembly in Northern Ireland.

Justis Parliament

Parlianet and *POLIS* were former databases of Parliamentary information and at one time POLIS was freely available on the Parliament website. That is no longer the case. Justis Publishing now provides *Justis Parliament* which has taken the *Parlianet/POLIS* content and added it to their subscription legal library. This service provides greatly enhanced searching capability compared to the information directly available on the Parliament website as well as access to the records of the Welsh and Northern Ireland Assemblies (*www.justis.com/justisparliament*). However, it is a subscription service.

Google and other search engines

Of course, many people rely on search engines and in particular Google to locate information and publications. For Parliamentary material using the advanced search in Google and delimiting the site option by 'publications. Parliament.uk' is an effective way of finding items.

ePolitix (*www.epolitix.com*) is produced by Dod's Parliamentary Communications Ltd, the publisher of various Parliamentary guides and the House Magazine (see below). It carries news, information about current bills, articles about people and in particular stakeholders and databases of stakeholders. These are the organisations such as Animal Defender International, Charity Commission and Woodland

Trust who will want to have a say in the decisions made by Parliament. ePolitix provides email news alerts and RSS feeds.

Dodonline (*www.dodonline.co.uk*) is also published by Dod's and provides biographical information about MPs and peers and constituency profiles. It is a subscription service but the very basic information, e.g. Party, constituency and majority, can be accessed free of charge. However, this information is readily available from the Parliament website. There is a printed alternative, *Dod's Parliamentary Companion,* published each year, and they also publish a *Constituency Guide.*

DeHavilland (*www.dehavilland.co.uk*) is a subscription service covering government, Parliament, devolved and European institutions, think-tanks, pressure groups, broadcasts, and political news and developments. Services include news alerts, select committee reports, conference reports, bespoke reports and a political helpdesk. The database also contains a significant media section covering UK media contacts in the national, regional, local and trade press. *DeHavilland* also offers profiles and biographies of political figures.

Gallery News (*www.gallerynews.co.uk*) is described as 'an interactive, real-time parliamentary and political news agency based in the House of Commons'. It is freely available to all parliamentarians and their staff and is available as a subscription service to others. It is based on press releases and comments emailed from politicians and carries reports on Lobby Briefings from Downing Street and a diary of political and parliamentary events.

Hansard Society (*www.hansard.org.uk*) is an independent political research and education charity with the aim of strengthening democracy. As such it researches and publishes on topics such as digital democracy, citizenship education and Parliamentary reform.

History of Parliament (*www.histparl.ac.uk*) is a major academic project to create a scholarly reference work describing the members, constituencies and activities of the Parliament of England and the United Kingdom. The volumes either published or in preparation cover the House of Commons from 1386 to 1868 and the House of Lords from 1660 to 1832.

References

Note: Legislation is available on the Official Legislation website at *www.legislation.gov.uk* and is not listed here.

Butcher, David (1991) *Official Publications in Britain*, 2nd edn. London: Library Association Publishing.

Erskine May's Parliamentary Practice: Treatise on the Law, Privileges, Proceedings and Usage of Parliament, 23rd edn (2004), eds Sir William Mckay, Frank Cranmer, Mark Hutton, Simon Patrick, Mary Robertson and Alan Sandell. London: Butterworths.

House of Commons Information Office Factsheet L1: covers the *Parliamentary Stages of a Government Bill*.

House of Commons Information Office Factsheets L3: *The Success of Private Members' Bills*.

House of Commons Information Office Factsheet L4: *Private Bills*.

House of Commons Information Office Factsheet L5: *Hybrid Bills*.

House of Commons Information Office Factsheet L7: *Statutory Instruments*.

House of Commons Information Office Factsheet L10: *Church of England Measures*.

House of Commons Information Office Factsheet P1: *Parliamentary Questions.*

House of Commons Information Office Factsheet P2: *Departmental Select Committees.*

House of Commons Information Office Factsheet P3: *Early Day Motions.*

House of Commons Information Office Factsheet P4: *Sittings of the House.*

House of Commons Information Office Factsheet P9: *Divisions.*

House of Commons Information Office Factsheet P17: *Guide to the Weekly Information Bulletin.*

House of Commons Information Office Factsheets L2: *Private Members' Bill Procedure.*

House of Lords Briefing. The Work of the House of Lords – Its Role, Functions and Powers (2009) Online at: *www. parliament.uk/documents/upload/HofLBprolefunctions. pdf.*

'UK Statute Law Database: First Impressions' (2007) *Refer*, 23(1): 15–20.

4

Devolved Parliament and Assemblies and regional government

This chapter covers:

- introduction to the devolved Parliament and Assemblies;
- Scotland:
  - structure and functions
  - publications and information
  - visiting the Scottish Parliament;
- Wales:
  - structure and functions
  - publications and information
  - visiting the National Assembly of Wales;
- Northern Ireland:
  - structure and functions
  - publications and information
  - visiting the Northern Ireland Assembly;
- regional government:
  - structure
  - publications.

Introduction to the devolved Parliament and Assemblies

There have been earlier devolution episodes but in this context the discussion is restricted to the devolution of power from Westminster to Scotland, Wales and Northern Ireland that has taken place over the past ten years. It was brought about by separate acts of Parliament for each body passed in 1998. The devolved legislatures are subordinate to the UK Parliament and, theoretically at least, the devolution of power could be reversed.

Scotland

The Scotland Act 1998 paved the way for the election of the first Scottish Parliament (SP) since 1707. Elections took place on 6 May 1999 and the SP was formally opened on 1 July 1999. Elections are held every four years.

The UK government's approach to devolution was, in effect, to say that any area that the 1998 Act did not reserve to Westminster was devolved.

'Reserved matters' are those where the responsibility for passing laws remains with the UK Parliament at Westminster because they are areas where the legislation will have an impact on the UK or internationally. These 'reserved matters' include financial and economic issues, trade, foreign affairs, defence and social security. This means that the Scottish Parliament has the power to legislate in most areas that affect the people of Scotland from education, health, prisons, local government, criminal justice, housing, arts, fisheries and more.

Structure and functions

The Scottish Parliament (SP)

The SP is made up of 129 Members of the Scottish Parliament (MSPs) who elect a Presiding Officer and two Deputy Presiding Officers who must then act impartially. It normally meets in plenary on Wednesday afternoons and all day Thursdays.

The role of the Scottish Parliament is to make laws in the devolved areas as described above and to scrutinise the work of the Scottish Executive or Scottish Government as it has been known since 2007. As in the Parliament at Westminster, it is also a forum for debate on important issues. In Scotland issues to be debated and considered by the SP can be raised by any individual, community group or organisation. This is done by submitting petitions to the Public Petitions Committee. The Public Petitions Committee is the body which decides whether or not a petition is admissible and what action should be taken. Petitions are also accepted electronically and information about the process is made available through a video and a podcast as well as leaflets which are posted to the web as pdfs and available in English and seven other languages. There have been nearly 500 e-petitions submitted since 2000 but more traditional petitions outstrip this with nearly 1,500 submitted by 2011. They are all listed on the website as open or closed, and a blog by the Public Petitions Committee describes in a very accessible style what the committee is discussing and how it operates. Petitions have been submitted on a vast array of subjects from the closure of coastguard stations to prohibiting the resale of football tickets and improved mobile phone coverage.

The SP website (*www.scottish.parliament.uk*) provides live coverage of the meetings of Parliament and committees, and a film archive is available for one month after the date of the meeting. The website also carries video podcasts called *Holyrood Highlights Weekly* looking at the major issues covered in the preceding month and providing a useful round-up of the business.

Committees of the Scottish Parliament

As in Westminster, the SP has committees whose role lies in 'scrutinising legislation, conducting inquiries, gathering evidence and holding the Scottish Government (previously the Scottish Executive) to account'. The website contains a detailed guide to their work and structure, how to follow the proceedings, how the room is set up, who attends and what to expect if attending or watching a televised committee. The leaflet even tells you who designed the carpets and the technique used to print the pattern!

There are Mandatory Committees and Subject Committees with the option to set up temporary committees to tackle a particular issue if this is felt to be appropriate.

Mandatory Committees and *Subject Committees* are set up at the beginning of a Parliamentary Session and for the 2007–11 Session were

- Audit (which became the Public Audit Committee in 2008)
- Economy, Energy and Tourism
- Education, Lifelong Learning and Culture
- Equal Opportunities
- European and External Relations
- Finance
- Health and Sport
- Justice

- Local Government and Communities
- Procedures (replaced by Standards, Procedures and Public Appointments)
- Public Petitions
- Rural Affairs and Environment
- Standards and Public Appointments (replaced by Standards, Procedures and Public Appointments)
- Standards, Procedures and Public Appointments
- Subordinate Legislation
- Transport, Infrastructure and Climate Change.

Committees usually consist of between five and 15 MSPs, having regard to the balance of the parties in the SP, and it is the SP that approves nominations for each committee. Each committee has a convenor to chair meetings and is supported by a small team of clerks and committee assistants. The committee balance is calculated using the D'Hont method. Named after a Belgian mathematician, this is a mathematical way of allocating seats and it is also used for the allocation of convenerships.

These committees are noteworthy in that they combine the roles of Westminster's select and general committees. They scrutinise proposed legislation as well as conducting inquiries. A major difference between Westminster and the SP is that the committees are allowed to initiate legislation.

The website gives the current membership and the business of each committee. Committees normally meet weekly or fortnightly on Tuesday and Wednesday mornings and proceedings are webcast on *holyrood.tv* on the SP website. Some meetings take place away from Holyrood and most meetings are public. If you wish to attend a meeting, check the procedure on the website or call the SP (see below).

The work of the committees includes:

- scrutiny of the work of the Scottish Government;
- scrutiny of a proposal or draft bill;
- consideration of a bill;
- consideration of subordinate legislation;
- consideration of proposals for Members' bills;
- investigation of activities within the committee's remit.

Each committee is required to produce an annual report which has a word limit of 1,500 and publication is coordinated to ensure that all reports are published in the same week. The committees also, of course, publish reports of their findings and these are best found by visiting the section on the website for the relevant committee.

For further information see:

- *The Work of Committees of the Scottish Parliament (www.scottish.parliament.uk/vli/committees/documents/WOC-Eng.pdf)*
- *Guidance on Committees (www.scottish.parliament.uk/business/ParliamentaryProcedure/g-committee/cg-c.htm).*

The SP website at *www.scottish.parliament.uk* also lists details of committees that are no longer in operation from previous Parliamentary sessions.

The Scottish Government

The Scottish Government is a separate entity but as with the UK Parliament and government it is made up of Members of the Scottish Parliament (MSPs) from the majority party or parties, led by the First Minister who appoints a ministerial team. In addition the Government includes the two Scottish

Law Officers, the Lord Advocate and the Solicitor General, who are not required to be MSPs.

From 1999 until the 2007 election, Scotland was led by a Labour–Liberal Democrat coalition. Following the 2007 election and the formation of the Scottish National Party (SNP) administration, First Minister Alex Salmond renamed the 'Scottish Executive' the 'Scottish Government'. The Scottish Government is led by the First Minister, who is nominated following a vote by MSPs and is appointed by the Queen on the recommendation of the Presiding Officer.

The Scottish Government is supported by what was the Scottish Office and staff remain UK civil servants although accountable to Scottish ministers.

The Scottish Government website is at *www.scotland.gov. uk*. Information about the work of the Scottish Government can mainly be found under 'Topics' on the website. The areas covered include agriculture, business and industry, education and training, rural development and sport, and there is no need to know or understand the structure of the organisation to be able to access the information.

Publications and information

From an information viewpoint, the SP's policy is a model of how a legislative or indeed any official body should publish. The SP publishes both in print and digital formats. In addition, it offers an external information service through its 'Partner Library' network. Each Scottish local authority was asked to nominate its most suitable library to hold a collection of SP publications – in effect creating a network of SP publication centres. A full-time member of the SP staff acts as a liaison officer, offering advice and training in the use of SP publications and information. There is a 'Partner Library' page on the Scottish Parliament website that lists the addresses of the partner libraries (*www.scottish.parliament. uk/vli/partners/libraries/index.htm*).

Seaton writing in *Refer* in 1999 covers the background to SP publishing and its information strategy. The strategy was originally developed by the Consultative Steering Group on the Scottish Parliament and their report of January 1999 included a draft information strategy. This strategy was unusual for the time as it set out not only how the Parliament was to provide information to the public but how this information would ensure that citizens were well-informed and could therefore contribute to the democratic process. Alongside this was recognised the need for well-informed MSPs so that they could 'contribute fully to the governance of Scotland'.

The resulting structure was the provision of external information services through the Public Information Service and the Education Services, and an internal information service through the Scottish Parliament Information Centre (SPICe).

Initially TSO managed publishing for the SP but in 2004 the contract was let to Astron (now called R.R. Donnelley). Only Scottish Acts and Statutory Instruments, publication of which is the responsibility of the Queen's Printer for Scotland, still appear in the *Daily List* published by TSO.

SPICe

The Scottish Parliament Information Centre (SPICe) produces much useful background material on SP issues. It provides an enquiry service, factsheets, information on the history of the SP and impartial briefings for MSPs on many aspects of the SP's work, and all of this information is available on the website. SPICe publishes research briefings on current bills and these can be found on the webpage for the bill in question.

Business Bulletin

The Business Bulletin's coverage is similar to that of Westminster's Vote Bundle in that it covers the current day's business and future business of the SP. It includes committee agendas, details of oral questions and questions for written answers, motions and amendments, new bills and new amendments to bills, and details of new documents laid before Parliament (including new petitions) together with new Committee Reports. The Bulletin also details the progress of legislation. The Bulletin is produced daily while the SP is in session and weekly when the Parliament is in recess. An archive is available on the website from 1999. It contains:

- Announcements
- Section A: Daily Business List
- Section B: Business Programme
- Section C: Agendas of Committee Meetings
- Section D: Oral Questions
- Section E: Written Questions
- Section F: Motions and Amendments
- Section G: Bills
- Section H: Documents laid
- Section I: Petitions lodged
- Section J: Progress of Parliamentary Business.

The website carries a Calendar of Parliamentary Events covering the forthcoming month and this can be reached from the link to 'This week in the Scottish Parliament'. *What's Happening in the Scottish Parliament* (WHISP) preceded the calendar and for historical information there is an archive of WHISP publications on the site (*www.scottish. parliament.uk/vli/history/whisp/index*).

Official Report

The equivalent of *Hansard* for the SP is known as the *Official Report* and covers all the business of the Parliament and its committees.

The *Official Report* is published in several series:

- Plenary – the record of the meetings of the SP;
- Written Answers Report – containing written answers to Parliamentary questions;
- Committee – the record of the proceedings (including evidence sessions) of the committees.

The 'Plenary' series covers similar material to Westminster's *Hansard*: debates, statements and oral questions. Most MSPs' contributions are in English but some are in Gaelic and these are accompanied by a translation into English. Like *Hansard*, the *Official Report* is substantially verbatim. It is available on the website by 8am on the morning after the plenary session, and a schedule of publication appears on the website giving the date of the meeting, date of publication of the report and date of the next meeting.

Reports of committee meetings are usually published before the next meeting of that committee. Printed copies can be purchased from:

Blackwell's Bookshop
53 South Bridge
Edinburgh
EH1 1YS
Tel: 0131 622 8222

Minutes of proceedings

These are the formal record of each meeting of the SP, listing all items of business considered together with a record of any decisions and votes. They appear on the website the day after the meeting.

Journal of Parliamentary Proceedings

The *Journal of Parliamentary Proceedings* contains 'the minutes of chamber proceedings, notices of bills, instruments and draft instruments, reports of committees, and other matters which the Parliament considers should be included'. It is the authoritative record of what the Parliament has done and is published every Parliamentary year.

Bills

A list of current bills appears on the SP website. Each bill has a page which provides a one-stop shop for information on the progress of the bill. The bill page includes links to all the relevant documents, including the Lead Committee's consideration, the SPICe bill briefing and all the versions of the bill.

The progress of bills through the Scottish Parliament can be tracked through the Scottish Parliament website where they are listed alphabetically and the progress is set out on a chart called the Current Bill Tracker. A link gives basic information about the bill and links to the text of the bill, the accompanying Explanatory Notes and Policy Memorandum and Delegated Powers Memorandum. (A Delegated Powers Memorandum sets out the powers which a bill intends to delegate and to which bodies.)

Acts and Statutory Instruments

Acts of the Scottish Parliament (ASPs) are published under the 'authority and superintendence of the Queen's Printer for Scotland' and printed by TSO. All acts passed by the SP are available on the *www.legislation.gov.uk* alongside the legislation for the UK, Wales and Northern Ireland.

They have been accompanied by Explanatory Notes from the first in 1999.

Scottish Statutory Instruments (SSIs) are made under the authority of acts of the Scottish Parliament and may also be accompanied by Executive Notes. They are also available on *www.legislation.gov.uk*.

Other publications

The *Scottish Parliament Bibliography* is an annual publication which lists all the publications of the SP, documents scrutinised by the SP and statutory publications including Acts and SSIs. An archive is available on the website (*www. scottish.parliament.uk/corporate/bibliographies/index.htm*).

SPICe factsheets are produced listing the current SP publications and documents laid before the SP and these cumulate from the date of publication of the last Bibliography and are updated weekly. Full bibliographies are published for each Parliamentary session.

The *Scottish Parliament Statistics* volumes provide factual information on all aspects of Parliamentary business and are very useful publications. There has been a break in publication of this series but it is intended that publication should resume.

The SP also publishes an *Annual Report* as does the Scottish Parliamentary Corporate Body. These offer useful background to the work and the philosophy of the SP.

Further information

One of the advantages of a new Parliament created in a digital age is that pretty well all the information about how it works and what it is doing has been made available electronically from day one. However, when comparing it with the website of Parliament at Westminster it is noticeable how much of the information available is in the form of e-booklets and e-publications rather than simply pages of web content.

Visiting the Scottish Parliament

Access to the new Parliament building in Edinburgh is free and visitors are encouraged and welcomed. There is an exhibition and shop as well as access to the public galleries of the Chamber and the Committee Rooms. To book tickets for the gallery and to check ahead of visiting the building, go to the website or check with:

> Visitor Services
> The Scottish Parliament
> Edinburgh
> EH99 1SP
> Tel: 0131 348 5200
> Text: 0131 558 7676
> Fax: 0131 348 5601
> Email: *sp.bookings@scottish.Parliament.uk*

Scottish Parliament

The powers of the Parliament, elections, law-making, how parliament works, and relations with Westminster, local government and Europe are covered in *The Scottish Parliament: An Introduction* by McFadden and Lazarowicz (2010).

The first decade of the Scottish Parliament, devolution, SP committees, legislative process, elections and wider issues are discussed in Jeffrey and Mitchell (2009).

How the Scottish Parliament Works

How the Scottish Parliament Works is a series of booklets available at *www.scottish.parliament.uk*. The series offers useful information on many aspects of the SP, including details of procedure and the work of MSPs. These are also available as print versions from the Public Information Service at:

The Scottish Parliament
Edinburgh
EH99 1SP
Tel: 0131 348 5000
Fax: 0131 348 5601
Email: *sp.info@scottish.parliament.uk*

Scottish Government

Publications of the Scottish Government are listed at *www. scotland.gov.uk/publications* and can be searched by date or keyword or viewed by category from a selection of categories. More than 1,000 publications are issued by the Scottish Government each year and the web page can be supplied as an RSS feed to help in keeping track of new publications.

A monthly list is produced by R. R. Donnelley giving details of the publications issued that month that are only available on the web. This list can be found by going to the SWOP website at *www.lib.gla.ac.uk/swop* (see below).

InfoScotland

There is a Scottish Government site dedicated to initiatives called *InfoScotland* which brings together information about campaigns such as those around creating a healthier Scotland and a safer Scotland (*www.infoscotland.com*).

Scotland: the official online gateway

www.scotland.org is aimed at anyone wanting to visit Scotland to work, study, do business or just take a holiday. It carries extensive information about the country including useful facts and figures.

The Scottish Working Group on Official Publications (SWOP)

SWOP (*www.lib.gla.ac.uk/swop*), which is affiliated to the Scottish Confederation of University and Research Libraries (SCURL), works 'to increase awareness of, and access to, official publications, and to encourage best practice in the production, dissemination and use of official information'. Articles on their work and developments in access to Scottish official information appear in *Refer* (and the supporting website *referplus*), the journal of the Information Services Group of CILIP *http://sites.google.com/site/referplus/* SWOP is also represented on the Standing Committee on Official Publications (SCOOP) where issues related to access to official publications across the UK are discussed. (See *www.cilip.org.uk* and follow the links to Special Interest Groups and the Information Services Group for more information on the work of SCOOP.)

The National Library of Scotland

The National Library of Scotland as a deposit library holds the largest collection of Scottish official publications in Scotland, and the Official Publications Unit operates a blog which offers a rather different look at official publications.

Wales

The Government of Wales Act 1998 devolved power to the National Assembly for Wales. Unlike the Scottish Parliament, only policy areas specified in the legislation were devolved to Wales; all other policy areas remained the responsibility of Westminster. It was intended that it should provide a single body which would combine debate and decision-making. In practice this model resulted in problems between the decision-makers and the wider assembly. The report of a Commission led by Lord Richard of Ammanford which had been set up in 2002 to review 'the powers and electoral arrangements of the National Assembly in order to ensure that it was able to operate in the best interests of the people of Wales' led to the Government of Wales Act 2006 (GOWA).

Under the 2006 Act the legislative powers of the Assembly were enhanced, giving the Assembly the power to create primary legislation for the first time, albeit via Westminster. The Assembly must ask Westminster for 'legislative competence' in an area of legislation and once that has been granted will make 'Assembly measures' which will in effect be Acts. Examples include:

- *the NHS Redress (Wales) Measure 2008* which allowed 'Welsh Ministers to make regulations for the NHS in Wales so that they can settle certain clinical negligence claims locally without the need for legal action';

- *the Social Care Charges (Wales) Measure 2010* which provided for a fairer and more consistent approach to charging for non-residential social services across Wales.

The roles of the legislature (the National Assembly for Wales) and the executive (the Welsh Assembly Government) were also formally separated.

Structure and functions

The National Assembly for Wales

The National Assembly for Wales has 60 members known as Assembly Members (AMs) and they are elected every four years using the 'first past the post' system as at Westminster for local constituency members and a proportional representation system for the election of regional members. A Presiding Officer is elected at the first meeting after the election of the Assembly and chairs the Plenary, taking the same role as the Speaker in the House of Commons. The full meetings of the Assembly are held on Tuesday and Wednesday afternoons in the Siambr or Chamber.

The role of the National Assembly for Wales is to scrutinise and monitor the decisions and policies of Welsh Ministers and hold Ministers to account by:

- approving budgets for the Welsh Assembly Government;
- examining and approving Assembly Measures;
- approving certain subordinate legislation;
- advising on the appointment of the Auditor General for Wales and the Public Service Ombudsman;
- receiving reports, e.g. from the Auditor General.

Individual Assembly Members or Assembly committees can also propose Assembly Measures or legislation.

The Assembly has several committees dealing with the following issues:

- Communities and Culture Committee
- Enterprise and Learning Committee
- Health, Wellbeing and Local Government Committee
- Sustainability Committee

- Business Committee
- Children and Young People Committee
- Equality of Opportunity Committee
- European and External Affairs Committee
- Finance Committee
- Petitions Committee
- Public Accounts Committee
- Scrutiny of First Minister
- Committee on Standards of Conduct.

Committees are also appointed to consider legislation.

Welsh Assembly Government

The Welsh Assembly Government consists of a First Minister who is nominated by the Assembly and then appointed by the Queen. The First Minister appoints up to 12 Welsh Ministers and Deputy Ministers and seeks the Queen's approval for these appointments. The First Minister also appoints a Counsel General, the equivalent of the Attorney General, whose role is to advise on legal and constitutional matters. Due to the proportional representational element in the electoral system no party has secured an overall majority in the Assembly. There have been two periods of minority government by the Labour Party (1999–2000 and 2003–07) and two coalition governments (Labour and Liberal Democrat 2000–03 and Labour and Plaid Cymru 2007–11). Labour won sufficient seats in the May 2011 (30 out of 60) to form a government.

The Welsh Assembly Government is responsible for decision-making, developing and implementing policy, exercising statutory functions and duties, making subordinate legislation and proposing Assembly Measures. Its policy remit covers most areas including:

- agriculture
- fisheries
- forestry
- rural development
- culture
- local government
- public administration
- social welfare
- sport and recreation
- economic development
- health and health services
- highways and transport
- the Welsh language
- housing
- tourism
- town and country planning
- water and flood defence.

Publications and information

The National Assembly for Wales publications

The website for the National Assembly for Wales is at *www.assemblywales.org.*

All Assembly publications are made available in both English and Welsh and the website allows users to select the language they wish to use from the home page. You can select to view the website in English or Welsh.

Business of the Assembly

The *Business Notice* webpage gives details of all Plenary and Committee meetings for the current and following week as well as details of the most recent business tabled or laid before the Assembly including motions, questions and legislation. The *Business Notice* posted on the Assembly website is for the current week only. Previous issues are available via the UK Web Archive at *www.webarchive.org. uk/ukwa.*

The pages cover Agendas, Oral Questions, Motions and Amendments, Votes and Proceedings, Future Business, Written Questions, Documents Laid and Statements of Opinions as well as links to previous Assembly sessions.

Official record

The primary source for the *Record of Proceedings* for the National Assembly for Wales is the website, as might be expected of an organisation created at a time when the web was already established. The Record is found by following the links to *Business* and then *Plenary* and it is split into that which covers the current Assembly and the record of proceedings of the First (1999–2003), Second (2003–2007) and Third (2007–2011) Assemblies. The Record of Proceedings is published within 24 hours of the end of the meetings held in the Chamber and transcripts are published in English and Welsh. The two versions are set out in columns side by side so that readers can see both versions together. In the *Votes and Proceedings* section a summary of the business can be found and this is issued within 30 minutes of the end of the meeting.

Welsh Assembly Government publications

Most Welsh Assembly Government publications are produced in print and electronic format. They cover topics such as agriculture, community safety, health care, housing, population, transport, indices of multiple deprivation and an extensive collection of statistical publications. Publications are available in both English and Welsh. Printed copies of publications may be ordered from the:

Publications Centre
Room 3.022
Welsh Assembly Government

Cathays Park
Cardiff
CF10 3NQ
Tel: 029 2082 3683
Fax: 029 2082 5239
Email: *wag-en@mailuk.custhelp.com*

On the website, documents and information are arranged by topic and quick links are provided to the latest and popular documents for those topics. Providing you understand that the publications are arranged by topic then you should be able to find what you need.

An example is the topic 'Business and Economy' which is split up into sub-categories such as 'Help for your business', 'Digital Wales' and 'Bringing your business to Wales'. Here you will find relevant information and publications. The final link under the sub-categories is publications and this takes you to a chronological list of publications on the topic but with a search facility as well.

If you fail to understand the topic structure the homepage link to 'publications' can be a little confusing because this is designed to provide access to items you cannot find on the website. It seems to be centred on the Publication Scheme but the link takes you to the model scheme on the site of the Information Commissioner's website rather than a specific scheme for the Welsh Assembly Government. In fact the link you need is to 'How to obtain a publication' and this will lead you to a catalogue of publications or information register which you can search by author, subject or title. Once you have found the catalogue entry you are required to request a copy from the Publication Centre rather than being able to download the document. To be fair, this is because it is designed to provide access to material not available on the website but it would be good to be able to access scanned versions as a minimum.

Also under 'publications' on the homepage there is a quick link to a section dedicated to strategy documents where the content is again divided up into categories such as business and economy, children and young people, culture and sport, local government, older people and planning. The emphasis is on current strategies and you will find, for instance, that the *Wales Transport Strategy* carries a note that says it supersedes the *Transport Framework for Wales* but there is no link to the Framework and you will need to return to the catalogue referred to above to request a copy.

Welsh Assembly Government publications are also distributed to 40 Information Link libraries across Wales with one copy of everything published in print by the Welsh Assembly Government deposited at each and they have to undertake to keep the publications for at least six months. The system is operated in partnership with the Public Library Authorities in Wales.

Welsh Assembly Government Circulars have been issued on a variety of topics such as safeguarding children – *WAGC 005/2008 – Safeguarding Children in Education: The Role of Local Authorities and Governing Bodies under the Education Act 2002* and the financial contingency fund as in *WAGC 012/2008 – Financial Contingency Fund 2008/09*. Until 2008 these appeared on the website as a separate section, arranged in sets by their year of publication. They are now listed under the relevant topic and are not brought together in one place as previously.

Legislation

The Government of Wales Act 2006 allows the National Assembly for Wales to make Assembly Measures in devolved policy areas, but only where specific legislative competence has been granted by Westminster. Legislative competence can be devolved to the Assembly either by Act of Parliament or by Legislative Competence Order (LCO). Both procedures modify schedule 5 to the Government of Wales Act 2006. Part 4 of the GOWA 2006 allows for legislative competence in devolved policy fields to be transferred to the Assembly subject to a referendum which took place in March 2011. If an appropriate Act of Parliament is expected, a clause conferring legislative competence on the Assembly may be included within the Act. Alternatively, the Welsh Assembly Government, an Assembly Committee or individual Assembly Member can propose a draft LCO, which needs to be approved by the Assembly and scrutinised and affirmed by both Houses of Parliament before legislative competence is transferred. The Assembly is then able to make measures within the specific legislative competence granted.

Acts of Parliament may also transfer executive powers and responsibilities to the Welsh Assembly Government without transferring corresponding legislative competence to the Assembly. LCOs have been made in areas such as affordable housing, organ donation, school governance and the Welsh language. In all, 16 orders were been laid before the Assembly between 2008 and 2011 with one withdrawn and 15 approved.

The National Assembly website tracks the process of LCOs and Assembly Measures and provides an up to date copy of schedule 5 to the GOWA 2006 showing the Assembly's legislative competence.

Further information

The National Assembly for Wales has established a Members' Research Service which provides a library service for Members and publishes a number of guides and briefings. There is an extensive set of *Topic Briefs* to help Assembly

Members to get to grips with many areas of the Assembly's business. There is also a set of *Quick Guides* which are short descriptions of processes and concepts and can help in understanding how the Assembly functions. They have been produced on topics such as various aspects of the constitution, budget and finance, economic development, transport and sustainability, and Europe. Although these are primarily produced for Assembly Members, they are freely available on the Assembly website and provide a very useful resource both to help in understanding how devolved government functions in Wales and in developing an understanding of the areas of responsibility it has.

Visiting the Welsh Assembly

The Welsh Assembly's Senedd is open to the public and offers exhibitions and refreshments as well as the chance to sit in on plenary sessions and the full meetings of the Assembly held on Tuesday and Wednesday afternoons in the Siambr (Chamber). Prospective visitors should check the website for details or

- telephone the Booking Line on 0845 010 5500;
- textphone 0845 010 5678;
- email *assembly.bookings@wales.gov.uk*;
- write to: Assembly Booking Service, National Assembly for Wales, North Wales Visitor Centre, Princes Park, Princes Drive, Colwyn Bay, Conwy LL29 8PL.

Northern Ireland

Northern Ireland had a Parliament from 1921 but the information here relates to the devolution of power since

1999. As with Scotland and Wales, powers were devolved from the UK Parliament at Westminster to a Northern Ireland Assembly and an Executive elected from its Members through a 1998 Act of Parliament. The Northern Ireland Act 1998 gave legislative form to the institutions set up under the terms of the Belfast Agreement signed on Good Friday 1998 and often referred to as the Good Friday Agreement. It established the current structure of government in Northern Ireland and the ways in which it would collaborate with the government in the United Kingdom and the Republic of Ireland. Its role is to scrutinise the work of the Northern Ireland Government Departments and to make legislation.

Under legislation preceding the Northern Ireland Act 1998 elections to the Assembly were held on 25 June 1998 and it met for the first time six days later on 1 July. Apart from a return to direct rule from Westminster from February to May 2000 and two one-day suspensions in 2001, this Executive continued in office until 2002. On that date the Assembly was again suspended and direct rule from Westminster reintroduced.

Fresh Assembly elections were held on 26 November 2003. The Members elected at this time did not meet until 15 May 2006, when they were given the specific remit of preparing for devolution as part of a revived process of negotiation. The St Andrews Agreement of 13 October 2006, which resulted from this process, paved the way for devolution. Elections were held on 7 March 2007 and a Northern Ireland Executive once more took office on 8 May 2007. It is clear from this that the passage of the transfer of power has been far from easy. In 2010 justice and policing powers were devolved from Westminster, the final part of the 1998 peace agreement.

Structure and functions

Northern Ireland Assembly

The Assembly consists of 108 members from 18 constituencies and the members are known as Members of the Legislative Assembly (MLAs). They are responsible for areas such as education, health, agriculture, policing and criminal law.

As with Scotland and Wales, there are matters of UK importance such as security and foreign policy which are described as 'excepted matters' and remain within the jurisdiction of the UK government.

The Assembly usually meets twice a week and, as at Westminster, the sessions are chaired by a Speaker elected by the Assembly Members.

The website for the Northern Ireland Assembly is at *www.niassembly.gov.uk.*

Northern Ireland Executive

The Northern Ireland Executive is a four-party executive committee, which consists of the First and Deputy First Ministers who, despite their titles are of equal standing, and the Ministers for each of the 10 government departments. The Executive can propose primary and secondary legislation. The government departments are responsible for the administration of public services including health, education and the environment, and the minister for each department is appointed from the 108 MLAs.

The website for the Northern Ireland Executive is at *www.northernireland.gov.uk.*

The Northern Ireland Assembly Commission is responsible for providing the Assembly with accommodation, staff and services. It is chaired by the Speaker and consists of five other Assembly Members.

Committees

The Northern Ireland Assembly has a number of Statutory Committees whose role is to 'advise and assist each Northern Ireland minister in the formulation of policy with respect to matters within his/her responsibilities as a minister'.

They have eleven members and their responsibility is to:

- consider and advise on departmental budgets and annual plans in the context of the overall budget allocation;
- consider relevant secondary legislation and take the Committee Stage of relevant primary legislation;
- call for persons and papers;
- initiate inquiries and make reports; and
- consider and advise on matters brought to the committee by its minister.

(www.niassembly.gov.uk/io/Statutory.htm)

The Assembly also has Standing Committees and ad hoc Committees. Standing Committees, as the name suggests, are permanent and are the:

- Assembly and Executive Review Committee
- Committee on Procedures
- Business Committee
- Public Accounts Committee
- Committee on Standards and Privileges
- Audit Committee.

Their functions and roles are set out in the Northern Ireland Act 1998.

Ad hoc committees as the name suggests are set up as required.

Each of the committees has web pages on the *www. niassembly.gov.uk* site which gives membership, minutes, minutes of evidence, reports, press releases, research and draft legislation for that committee. Visit the *This Week at the Assembly* page for details of committee meetings.

Publications and information

Northern Ireland Assembly

Official record

The official record of the proceedings of the Northern Ireland Assembly is known as the *Official Report of the Northern Ireland Assembly (Hansard)* and the Daily Part is published by 8.30am on the day following the sitting. The Bound Volume is published by TSO after every '10 or so sittings'.

The Assembly website contains records of the meetings of the Assembly back to 1998 arranged in order of the Bound Volume and thus by date. There are no column or page numbers so it is difficult to reference. There is a simple search available which enables you to search by any words, all words or exact phrase and to limit the search to the title. An advanced search is also available which can help to refine searches by limiting the search to sections of the site such as particular committees, *Hansard*, biographies of MLAs or Written Answers and by when the pages were last updated, so if you know the item you are seeking was published in the last week you can limit the search to content updated in that period only.

Questions for Oral Answers are published on the website each Wednesday morning and the answers appear in the Official Report. *Questions for Written Answers* are listed by date on the website and the answers are published in the *Written Answers Booklet* published on the website each

Monday morning. Any questions left unanswered at the end of each week are published at the same time in the *Consolidated List of Questions*.

Departmental, Standing and Ad hoc Committees each have their own website homepage detailing their responsibilities, membership, minutes of meetings, press releases, research papers, work programme and contact details for the clerk. Committee reports are also published in hard copy by TSO and details can be found through the TSO website.

There is a publication scheme on the website as required by the Freedom of Information Act but unlike the schemes of the government departments in Northern Ireland it is not a database of publications.

An RSS feed of information about the Assembly including order papers, oral and written questions, etc. is available to help in keeping track of Assembly business, and another web page and RSS feed provides details of just the current day's business. Live coverage of the debates and committee meetings is provided through the Assembly website and an option called *Listen again* provides audio recordings to download within 48 hours of the end of a meeting and until the next meeting's recording is available. A video archive of the Assembly Question Times can be viewed at *www.niassembly.gov.uk/videoarchive.htm* and copies of the audio and video coverage may be requested free of charge through *soundandvision@niassembly.gov.uk*.

Written Ministerial Statements were introduced in March 2009 and are published on the website as received as well as appear in the Daily Part of the *Official Report (Hansard)* and in the Bound Volume for the appropriate period.

Northern Ireland Executive

With just 12 government departments and a short digital history, the website for the Northern Ireland Executive is uncluttered and simple to use. It sets out the role of the Executive, contains the Ministerial Code and lists news releases, Ministerial Statements and publications. It links to the sites for each of the Departments along with the Office of the First Minister and the Deputy First Minister. These all have a consistent look and feel and the same convention is used for the URL for each department. In each case the initials are used, e.g. Department of Culture, Arts and Leisure (Northern Ireland) is *www.dcalni.gov.uk*. This is the advantage of starting from scratch compared to trying to impose consistency retrospectively as is the case with the UK government where websites have been developed independently of each other over many years.

The Executive Committee occasionally issues *Executive Statements* which are made on cross-departmental topics such as flooding or foot and mouth disease. These are available from a link on the home page.

Each government department has a freedom of information publication scheme which, unlike many schemes, acts as a database of publications, with most publications available as pdfs to download and contact details for publications which are not available electronically.

Other publications and information

Although the Irish Republic is outside the scope of this book, it is worth mentioning that there is a *North/South Ministerial Council* which looks at issues which have an impact across the border such as waterways and food safety and there is cross-border cooperation in transport, agriculture, education, health, environment and tourism. *The British-Irish Council* looks at cooperation between the United Kingdom, Ireland, the devolved institutions in Northern Ireland, Scotland and Wales and the Isle of Man, Jersey and Guernsey, particularly in areas such as the environment, tourism and transport. It doesn't appear to have it's own website but information may be found on *www.nidirect.gov.uk*

Further information

A set of leaflets on various aspects of the Assembly such as the Plenary Sessions, the Committee System, the Legislative Process for Public Bills and the Official Report are available on the Northern Ireland Assembly website at *www.niassembly.gov.uk.*

The *Northern Ireland Yearbook (northernirelandyearbook. com)*, published each year, provides a guide to the departments, agencies and local councils as well as the Assembly, its members and the committees of Northern Ireland.

The Northern Ireland Assembly Research and Library Service *www.niassembly.gov.uk/researchandlibrary* publishes constituency profiles for each of the 18 constituencies of Northern Ireland and a series of research papers on a variety of topics. They also manage and record all the deposited papers for the Assembly. As in Parliament at Westminster, these are the unpublished papers which are placed in the Library at the direction of the Speaker or a Minister in the Executive. They will usually provide information supporting the response to a question to the Assembly.

Visiting the Northern Ireland Assembly

Members of the public are welcome to visit the plenary meetings of the Assembly which are usually held on Mondays and Tuesdays. Further information about visiting can be found through:

■ Website: *www.niassembly.gov.uk*

- Tel: +44 (0) 28 9052 1333
- Email: *info.office@niassembly.gov.uk*

Regional government

Here you will find:

- background to regional government and regional economic development bodies;
- background, structure, functions and publications of the Greater London Authority.

Background to regional government in England

A description of regional government and bodies is included here for completeness, but the election of the Coalition government in May 2010 has led to the demise of this level of government. The move towards establishing regional government in England followed the devolution of the home nations and would have functioned through elected Regional Assemblies. These would have been created after referenda in each region but, when the first referendum was held in the North East in 2004, it showed clearly that there was no support for elected regional assemblies. No further referenda were held but in each of the eight regions of England voluntary regional chambers already existed made up of representatives of local government, business and other local bodies. By 2002 they had become known as Regional Assemblies.

Regional Assemblies

Regional Assemblies or Chambers initially came together to act as a focal point for considering issues of regional significance. Under the Regional Development Agencies Act 1998 they were designated as the representative regional bodies with responsibility for scrutinising the work of the Regional Development Agencies (RDAs). They covered the same geographic areas as the Government Offices and RDAs and their role was:

1. To be consulted by the RDAs when developing their Regional Economic Strategy.

2. To act as the Regional Planning Body with responsibility for developing the Regional Spatial Strategy which includes the Regional Transport Strategy and Regional Waste Strategy.

3. To produce other regional strategies such as a regional sustainable development framework.

4. To act as Regional Housing Boards producing Regional Housing Strategies.

Membership

Regional Assemblies were not elected but had to be representative of the region. Central government guidance recommended that they should consist of up to 70 per cent local authority members which includes the National Parks Authorities and at least 30 per cent of representatives of areas such as higher and further education, the Confederation of British Industry, the Trades Union Congress, chambers of commerce, the small business sector, parish and town councils, the National Health Service, voluntary organisations, Learning and Skills Council, regional cultural consortia, and rural and environmental groups.

In July 2007 a report, *Review of Sub-national Economic Development and Regeneration*, was issued by HM Treasury,

BERR and DCLG. The review proposed that the Regional Development Agencies (RDAs) become responsible for producing an integrated regional strategy and that Regional Assemblies in the 'current form and function' should cease to exist. The legislation covering the Assemblies is repealed as part of the Local Democracy, Economic Development and Construction Act 2009 but it is up to the membership to decide when they cease to meet. They were replaced by Leadership Boards but these too have now been scaled down.

Publications of the regions

The main publications of the regions were the Regional Spatial Strategies (RSS) which incorporated a Regional Transport Strategy and the Regional Housing Strategies. These were controversial documents and on 6 July 2010 the Secretary of State for Communities and Local Government revoked them with immediate effect although this decision has been challenged.

Regional Development Agencies (RDAs)

As the development of regional government did not progress as had been intended the focus of regional bodies has been on economic development and on the work of the Regional Development Agencies. RDAs were established under the same legislation which led to the creation of the Regional Assemblies. The Regional Development Agencies Act 1998 sets out their purposes as:

1. to further economic development and regeneration;
2. to promote business efficiency and competitiveness;
3. to promote employment;

4. to enhance the development and application of skills relevant to employment; and

5. to contribute to sustainable development.

Publications of the RDAs

Each of the RDAs developed and published a Regional Economic Strategy setting out a vision for the strategic development of the region for the next ten years and including details of the main priorities for development and the actions to deliver the vision. Information about them was brought together on one website at *www.englandsrdas.com* but they all have their own sites which are linked to this. Most of the RDAs have chosen names which reflect their role in promoting the region in which they are working.

The complete list is:

- Advantage West Midlands (*www.advantagewm.co.uk*)
- East Midlands Development Agency (*www.emda.org.uk*)
- East of England Development Agency (*www.eeda.org.uk*)
- Northwest England Development Agency (*www.nwda.co.uk*)
- One North East (*www.onenortheast.co.uk*)
- South East England Development Agency (*www.seeda.co.uk*)
- South West of England Development Agency (*www.southwestrda.org.uk*)
- Yorkshire Forward (*www.yorkshire-forward.com*)
- London Development Agency (*www.lda.gov.uk*).

The Coalition government announced plans as part of its emergency budget in June 2010 to abolish RDAs. Coordination of economic development is now provided through Local Enterprise Partnerships (LEPs) with the first

24 announced in October 2010. These are partnerships of private companies, local authorities and the voluntary sector who work together within their area and have powers over planning, infrastructure and inward investment.

It remains to be seen what information these new bodies produce and how they publish this information. Individual websites are appearing and it can only be hoped that these will be drawn together, perhaps through the Department of Communities and Local Government or through Directgov or Business Link.

As an example of how these bodies may work, the LEP for Coventry and Warwickshire quickly decided to investigate developing a new website designed to encourage people to visit the area. It had identified a number of other uncoordinated sites and particularly wanted to promote visits to the area linked to Olympic events which would benefit the local economy. Its aim was to join up the current work in this area across the private and public sector and provide a single point for accessing information about tourism in the sub-region.

Another part of the Coalition government plans to provide for economic development after the demise of the RDAs is the creation of enterprise zones where incentives such as simpler planning rules and lower taxes will be on offer. These should help to attract investment and therefore lead to improved employment opportunities and will be set up in areas considered to have high growth potential.

Regional development bodies in Scotland, Wales and Northern Ireland

Scotland

Scotland has two economic development agencies providing business support and training and learning programmes as well as helping with community and cultural projects. Scottish Enterprise covers southern Scotland while the other, the Highlands and Islands Enterprise, covers the remainder of the country. The services are actually delivered by Local Enterprise Councils of which there are nine for the Highlands and Islands Enterprise and 12 for the Scottish Enterprise area. Scottish Enterprise and the Highlands and Islands Enterprise are executive, non-departmental public bodies and are sponsored by the Scottish Government:

- Scottish Enterprise (*www.scottish-enterprise.com*)
- Highlands and Islands Enterprise (*www.hie.co.uk*).

Wales

A Welsh Development Agency (WDA) was established under the Welsh Development Agency Act 1997 but in 2006 the WDA was discontinued and its work became the responsibility of the Welsh Assembly Government's Department of Economy and Transport.

Northern Ireland

Similarly in Northern Ireland the Department of Enterprise, Trade and Investment is home to Invest NI which aims to attract businesses to Northern Ireland (*www.investni.com*).

Greater London Authority (GLA)

The GLA was established in 2000 as a strategic authority to tackle London-wide issues. It was the first time since the Greater London Council was abolished in 1986 that there had been an elected body for the whole of London. For a history of local government in the capital which has over the years passed through the hands of the London County Council (LCC) and the Greater London Council (GLC) see *www.london.gov.uk/london-life/city-government/history.jsp*.

Its responsibilities include transport, policing, fire and emergency services, economic development, planning, culture and the environment. The GLA consists of the London Assembly and the Mayor of London and a team of staff. The elected Mayor champions the capital, drawing up policies for London and working with the London boroughs to tackle the issues which affect the whole area. The role of the Assembly is to scrutinise the work of the Mayor, which it does through receiving his reports, holding a monthly oral questions session, consultation, and by examining his decisions and policies.

Structure

The London Assembly consists of 25 elected members. Of these, 11 are London-wide assembly members and 14 represent constituencies which are made up of between two and four boroughs. Providing two-thirds of them agree, they can amend the Mayor's budget. They question the Mayor each month at the Mayor's Question Time which is held in public.

The GLA is based in City Hall on the south bank of the Thames, close to Tower Bridge, and the building is open to the public from 8am to 8pm Monday to Friday. Many of the meetings are open to the public and residents can sign up to receive details of consultations by email and submit their opinions electronically.

The website for the Greater London Authority is at *www.london.gov.uk*.

The GLA Group consists of the core GLA (the Mayor, London Assembly and support staff) as well as Transport for London, the Metropolitan Police Authority, the London Fire and Emergency Planning Authority and the London Development Agency. Although these are independent organisations, the Mayor sets their budgets and appoints some of their board members so the relationship is close.

Transport for London (TfL)

(*www.tfl.gov.uk*)

TfL is responsible for transport across the city including buses, the Underground, taxis and the Docklands Light Railway, and also for planning for the future to ensure that growth of the city is catered for as far as transport is concerned.

Metropolitan Police Authority (MPA)

www.mpa.gov.uk

Policing in London is provided by the Metropolitan Police Service but the MPA oversees the service, setting targets, monitoring performance and accounting for the budget.

London Fire and Emergency Planning Authority

www.london-fire.gov.uk

The LFEPA is responsible for protecting Londoners from fire and other emergencies.

London Development Agency

www.lda.gov.uk

The LDA 'builds on London's existing strengths to increase prosperity for London's people, businesses and communities and to improve Londoners' health and access to equal opportunities'. It has a budget of over £400m a year and works to achieve its objective by creating jobs, promoting London as a place to live, work and visit and improving access to skills training.

Publications and information

Agendas, minutes and other papers from the London Assembly and the Assembly Committees can be found on the website along with live webcasts and an archive of webcasts of the meetings and of the Mayor's press conferences.

All GLA publications are made available on the website *www.london.gov.uk* and can be obtained from the Public Liaison Unit (PLU) – see below.

Because the GLA is a strategic authority it publishes policy and strategy documents, of which there are large numbers, and many reports and results of investigations. Publications are listed by date and by subject category, and they cover topics as diverse as managing the noise from tube station PA systems to avoid disturbing residents to tourism, the Olympics, mental health services in London and street prostitution.

An email newsletter, *London Assembly Update*, is published monthly. Subscription is free and it is designed to keep people up to date with the work of the Assembly.

Specialist library and information services are provided to the Mayor, Assembly Members, the GLA and the GLA group organisations as well as the officers and councillors of the London boroughs by the GLA Information Services. Their services are also available to other organisations and individuals on a subscription basis.

The Information Services section of the Greater London Authority maintains a major database of urban and social policy which contains many official publications, as well as other resources. *Urbaline* covers books, journal articles and news stories, and access is via subscription. More information is available from: *www.london.gov.uk/gla/information-services/index.jsp*.

A useful collection of leaflets on the way the GLA functions is available from the GLA, Public Liaison Unit, City Hall, The Queen's Walk, London SE1 2AA (email *mayor@london .gov.uk*) or on the website at *www.london.gov.uk* (tel 020 7983 4100, minicom 020 7983 4458, fax 020 7983 4057).

References

Note: Legislation is available on the Official Legislation website at *www.legislation.gov.uk* and is not listed here.

Scotland

Jeffrey, Charlie and Mitchell, James (eds) (2009) *The Scottish Parliament 1999–2009: The First Decade*. Edinburgh: Luath Press in association with the Hansard Society.

McFadden, Jean and Lazarowicz, Mark (2010) *The Scottish Parliament: An Introduction*, 4th edn. London: Bloomsbury Professional.

Picton, Howard (1999) 'Public access to information on the Scottish Parliament', *Refer*, 15(2): 1–7.

Scottish Office (1999) *Report of the Consultative Steering Group on the Scottish Parliament. Presented to the Secretary of State for Scotland*. TSO. Online at: *http:// openscotland.net/library/documents-w5/rcsg-04.htm*.

Seaton, Janet (1999) 'The Scottish Parliament's information strategy', *Refer*, 15(3): 9–14.

Northern Ireland

Woodman, George (2000) 'The Northern Ireland Assembly', in Valerie Nurcombe (ed.), *Parliaments and Assemblies of the British Isles*, Proceedings of a one-day seminar, 22 November 1999.

Woodman, George (2001) 'The legislative process in the Northern Ireland Assembly', *Legal Information Management*, 1: 43–5.

5

Central government departments at Westminster

This chapter covers:

- introduction;
- structure, role and functions;
- publications and information;
- key central government information resources;
- case studies.

Introduction

The role of central government is wide ranging and touches each one of us. We may not be particularly aware of its role in our daily lives but there are departments concerned with our health, education, transport, justice, security, defence, business, industry, the environment, social care, work and pensions. Central government works to improve the health of the nation, to secure our safety as we travel, to provide support for the economy by advising businesses and ensuring the country has the infrastructure it needs to be profitable, to improve educational standards by setting policies and standards, to protect our environment from pollution and the effects of climate change, to ensure provision is made for the elderly, to maintain national security and develop foreign policy, and much more.

Because the work of central government is so wide ranging and so important to every citizen, there is a wealth of information which must be communicated, informing each of us of our duties and rights. It is also necessary for information to be made available to ensure the government is subject to public scrutiny and held to account.

Government publishes:

- to consult – to seek advice on what it might do on a particular issue;
- to inform;
- to promulgate, e.g. laws, regulations, guidelines;
- to advertise, i.e. to publicise a particular service; and
- to warn, e.g. a drink-driving campaign at Christmas.

Structure, role and functions

Central government departments

The work of central government is diverse and the areas covered and the departments responsible for those areas will change as the country changes, as new issues arise and as ways are sought to improve the delivery of services and support of the Government. Some departments are less likely to change their names and areas of responsibility, such as HM Treasury, the Cabinet Office and the Ministry of Defence, but others come and go. For example, the Ministry of Justice (*www.justice.gov.uk*) was formed in 2007 bringing together the courts, prisons, the probation services and attendance centres, and work to reform the criminal justice system. The department is also 'responsible for making new laws, strengthening democracy, modernising the constitution and safeguarding human rights'. Previously this work was covered by the Department for Constitutional Affairs along with the National Offender Management Service (NOMS) and the Office for Criminal Justice Reform.

Similarly the Department for Energy and Climate Change (*www.decc.gov.uk*) was created in October 2008 to bring together energy policy which was previously the responsibility of the Department for Business, Enterprise and Regulatory Reform and work to mitigate the impact of climate change, which had until then rested with the Department for Environment, Food and Rural Affairs. This was in recognition of the scale of the problems faced as a result of climate change and the need to address this alongside the need to secure clean, safe, affordable energy.

The Coalition government which came to power in May 2010 has made many changes but the main one for central government departments was the return to a Department for Education (*www.education.gov.uk*) which replaced the Department for Children, Schools and Families.

It would be impossible here to consider the responsibilities and functions of every central government department and the work would quickly go out of date. Directgov (*www.direct. gov.uk*) is the best source of information, with an A–Z of central government and links to details of current government departments and previous names and areas of responsibility. If you do not know the name of the department, locate it by drilling down through the subject categories. Entries contain references to previous departments and explain any changes of name and responsibility. For instance, the entry for the Department of Energy and Climate Change described above contains the following explanation of its origins.

The Department of Energy and Climate Change (DECC) is a new government department which brings together the work of the Climate Change Group, previously housed within the Department for Environment, Food and Rural Affairs (Defra), with the Energy Group from the Department for Business, Enterprise and Regulatory Reform (BERR) which itself has been replaced.

Each entry on Directgov gives a brief description, contact details and a link to the department's website.

The Parliament website also carries a list maintained by the House of Commons Information Office and which they aim to update within one working day of changes being announced. It can be found by following links from the home page to MPs, Lords and offices and the Government and Opposition.

As at the end of June 2010 after the Coalition government had been in power for two months the list was as below:

- Attorney General's Office
- Office of the Advocate General for Scotland
- Department for Business, Innovation and Skills
- Cabinet Office
- Department for Communities and Local Government
- Department for Culture, Media and Sport
- Ministry of Defence
- Department for Education
- Department of Energy and Climate Change
- Department for Environment, Food and Rural Affairs
- Foreign and Commonwealth Office
- Government Equalities Office

- Department of Health
- Home Office
- Department for International Development
- Ministry of Justice
- Office of the Leader of the House of Commons
- Office of the Leader of the House of Lords
- Northern Ireland Office
- Privy Council Office
- Scotland Office
- Department for Transport
- HM Treasury
- Wales Office
- Department for Work and Pensions
- HM Household
- Second Church Estates Commissioner representing Church Commissioners

The shorthand 'Whitehall' is often used to describe the government machine which covers the departments, agencies and other bodies staffed by civil servants and other public servants, and led by ministers. Some government departments are responsible for the whole of the UK while others cover England and Wales and Scotland or just England and Wales or indeed just England. The Ministry of Defence, for instance, is responsible for the security of the UK as a whole while the Department of Health covers only England. Some changes have been as the result of devolution and the Welsh Office, as an example, became the Wales Office on 1 July 1999 with the establishment of the National Assembly for Wales. The responsibilities of other departments also changed as the devolved bodies were formed.

The political head of a central government department will be a government minister. In a large department there will also be junior ministers with responsibility for particular aspects of the department's work. For instance, the Department for Communities and Local Government currently has a Secretary of State for Communities but also a Minister of State (Decentralisation, Big Society, Planning Policy), a Minister of State (Housing and Local Government) and then three Parliamentary Under Secretaries of State.

The Department for Work and Pensions, similarly, has a Secretary of State and Minister of State for Employment and a Minister of State for Pensions, with just two Parliamentary Under Secretaries of State. Parliamentary Under Secretaries of State will still be addressed as Minister. Smaller departments have fewer Ministers and fewer Parliamentary Under Secretaries of State. The Secretary of State for a department is usually a member of the Cabinet.

Government departments are staffed by career civil servants. Currently there are around 500,000 civil servants but this is set to be reduced as the Coalition government reduces public spending. The size of the Civil Service and therefore of central government departments has fluctuated over the years as their responsibilities have extended into more areas, followed by moves to improve efficiency and cut costs. In recent years these economies have included moving staff out of London and providing for flexible and mobile working. Figures for the number of civil servants were first published for 1970 although they had been produced before that for internal and academic purposes. The Civil Service website (*www.civilservice.gov.uk*) provides access to the statistical reports back to 1970. A total of 70 per cent of civil servants work in four departments which are the Department for Work and Pensions, the Home Office, the Ministry of Defence and HM Revenue and Customs.

The *Civil Service Yearbook* recorded the structure of the Service and the identities and roles of the more senior civil servants. Published each year for nearly 50 years by TSO as a large printed volume and in recent years accompanied by a CD-ROM version, it was inevitable with such a large organisation that this would very quickly go out of date. A web version was launched but even this was only updated twice a year. A live site with more frequent and speedier updating had been planned but has now ceased to exist and government departments are releasing organisational information through data.gov.uk. The problem with this is that there is no consistency in the way the information is made available and it is displayed in the order in which it is added and arranged by department or nation. A search may find you the data set you need but you would be unlikely to be able to navigate to the information by department as you are simply presented with a list of files, and as the list grows this will become even more difficult. Most departments will make their staff and structure available on their departmental websites but without the *Civil Service Yearbook* or a similar publication that brings the information for all departments together in one place it is difficult, for instance, to make comparisons between departments. *Dod's Civil Service Companion* provides contact details and biographies for about 4,000 civil servants so goes some way to filling the gap, although its price tag of more than £200 will not make it accessible to many.

Examples of departments, their functions and publications

A few examples have been picked out to give some indication of the functions of central government departments and what types of information they publish.

Department for Communities and Local Government

(*www.communities.gov.uk*)

The Department for Communities and Local Government has a wide remit. Its areas of responsibility include planning, local government, housing, fire and anti-social behaviour. As such it issues information and guidance on an array of topics. It is the latest in a long line of departments which have had responsibility for these aspects of government, and tracing information about the government departments which preceded it can be difficult. It is aided by the National Archives who manage the archiving of government websites, and by the Directgov website which gives information about some former departments.

The types of publications produced by the department include research and statistics, policy guidance, e.g. Planning Policy Statements, Building Regulations, Circulars on fire and rescue issues and other topics, leaflets, manuals and consultations (see review of the website below).

Department for Education

(*www.education.gov.uk*)

The Department for Education replaced the Department for Children, Schools and Families (DCSF) in 2010 which in turn had replaced the Department for Education and Skills in 2007, though some responsibilities went to other departments. It is responsible for education and children's services.

It is a good example of the impact of a change in government on the official publications of a department.

The DCSF published a number of strategies and action plans such as the strategy for tackling teenage pregnancy, guidance on topics such as supporting young people with learning difficulties, research and statistics.

Where information has been moved across to the new website for the new department much of it carries a warning that 'This page may not reflect Government policy'.

A link to publications is provided from the 'Menu' button and this provides access to publications by date, by topic, by new and popular publications and via a search. An archive is included, which is essential with the departmental changes which have taken place, and a facility to store items downloaded for convenient access in future.

Department for Work and Pensions

(*www.dwp.gov.uk*)

The Department for Work and Pensions (DWP) is responsible for providing support and advice to people of working age, employers, disabled people, pensioners, families and children. It is one of the largest government departments according to the ONS and it publishes policy documents, guidance on topics such as benefits and impact assessments which seek to show the impact of changes in policy in this area as well as large numbers of leaflets explaining benefits and services available to those with particular needs.

Department for Business, Innovation and Skills

(*www.bis.gov.uk*)

The Department for Business, Innovation and Skills was created in June 2009 from a merger of the Department for Business, Enterprise and Regulatory Reform (BERR) and the Department for Innovation, Universities and Skills (DIUS). It is responsible 'for enterprise, business relations, regional development and fair markets, along with responsibility for science and innovation, further and higher education and skills'.

It publishes information that will help businesses, including guidance on business law and business sectors, consumer issues and skills for business. The website also carries the publications for:

- UK Trade & Investment (UKTI)
- The Insolvency Service.

HM Treasury

(*www.hm-treasury.gov.uk*)

The Treasury is responsible for economics and finance and its aim is to 'raise the rate of sustainable growth, and achieve rising prosperity and a better quality of life with economic and employment opportunities for all'.

The Treasury publishes the many documents which communicate the detail of the budget and spending reviews as well as economic data in the form of the Pocket Data Book, a weekly set of economic indicators for domestic and international economies and other statistics and economic forecasts. Its website is heavily used when budget or comprehensive spending review announcements are made.

Non-ministerial departments

Non-ministerial departments are departments which are not headed by a minister but by a permanent office holder. Currently (January 2010) they include bodies such as:

- Charity Commission for England and Wales
- Crown Estate

- Office of Fair Trading
- Serious Fraud Office.

These bodies are detailed in the List of Ministerial Responsibilities including Executive Agencies and Non Ministerial Departments on the Cabinet Office website at *http://www.cabinetoffice.gov.uk/media/416777/lmr100701.pdf*.

> Non-ministerial departments (NMDs) are departments in their own right, established to deliver a specific function; part of government, but independent of Ministers. The precise nature of relationships between NMDs and Ministers vary according to the individual policy and statutory frameworks, but the general rationale is to remove day-to-day administration from ministerial control. (Select Committee on Treasury, Tenth Report, 18 July 2006.)

As with government departments there is a requirement to make information available to the citizen.

Publications and information

Central government publications, as we have seen from the examples above, include

- Green Papers for consultation
- White Papers setting out the Government's view on a topic
- press releases
- maps
- statistics

- reports
- public information leaflets
- speeches and much more.

The publication of information has grown and extended over the past century, particularly since the Second World War, matching the growth of government. The emergence of the web and digital technologies has accelerated this growth still further and made the information far more accessible to the general population providing they have web access and the necessary skills. The election of the Coalition government in May 2010 has similarly stepped up the publication of information, with departments now required to publish their Business Plans. The Department for Communities and Local Government, for instance, published its Business Plan for 2011–15 in November 2010 setting out that it will undertake a radical reform of the planning system to give people and communities 'far more ability to determine the shape of the places in which they live', reform the Community Infrastructure Levy, provide funding to help town and parish councils to develop neighbourhood plans, publish new designations to protect areas of importance to local communities, publish new Energy National Policy Statements and replace the Infrastructure Planning Commission with a Major Infrastructure Planning Unit. These and other plans are set out with target dates with the intention that the department can be held to account on its delivery against this plan.

Command Papers

Some departmental publications are issued as Command Papers, the role and numbering of which has been described in Chapter 3 on Parliament at Westminster because they are 'presented to Parliament'. The National Archives publishes guidance for departments on what is a Command Paper and how they should be published and presented to Parliament. The document gives the following checklist for deciding whether or not a publication should be a Command Paper and it is reproduced here as it provides a useful guide to what Command Papers are.

(a) Is it going to prompt an Oral Statement in the House?

(b) Is it of constitutional importance?

(c) Is it a consultation paper on proposed policies which might lead to future primary legislation (e.g. a Draft Bill) or a significant piece of delegated legislation? and

(d) Does the document set out policies which might form the basis for a subsequent debate by either House?

(e) Will there be future interest in finding the document and where archiving as part of the sets of Parliamentary Papers will therefore be useful?

If the answer to any one of these is 'Yes' then the document ought to be published as a Command Paper. However, in practice, for most departments only a very small proportion of their output appears as Command Papers.

This means that many of the types of publications listed above such as Green Papers, White Papers and reports should be published as Command Papers. The terms White and Green Paper are not used in the titles of the publications themselves as they are considered to be informal descriptions and do not have an official definition. They will be numbered as described in Chapter 3 and printed, usually by TSO, and then arrangements made to present them to Parliament. This may be through an oral or a written statement, and only when this has happened can they be made publicly available. The process requires careful management, timing and consultation with numerous people.

All Command Papers are published on the Official Documents website (*http://www.official-documents.gov.uk/*).

Consultations

The government often needs to consult the public on matters of policy and it will publish a consultation document or Green Paper, set out a process for responses, set a deadline for those responses and publish the findings. Keeping track of what is being consulted on and the closing date for responses is important for many people and in the digital age there are a number of ways to do this. Efforts are being made not only to use technology to alert people to the launch of a consultation but also to engage them in the consultation process through in particular the use of social media tools and to make them aware of the closing date for a consultation.

When a consultation is launched a Command Paper may be published with an oral or written statement made in the House of Commons or the Lords. The publication of the document will be listed in the *TSO Daily List* and the written or oral statement recorded in *Hansard*. If the consultation is high profile there will be a press conference and press notices will be issued. This means that there will be press coverage. The details will be listed on the website of the issuing department and you should be able to sign up to an RSS feed on these sites to alert you to publication of a consultation.

The electronic alerting service Wired-gov (*www.wired-gov.net*) provides an email alerting service in conjunction with the Central Office of Information and many other organisations in central government and the wider public sector. It is free to the public sector and on subscription to the private sector. It includes details of consultations and can be used to alert you to new consultations and approaching deadlines for responses.

Similarly the website and email alerting service run by Communities and Local Government but working with other departments, agencies and public bodies *info4local.gov.uk* (*www.info4local.gov.uk*) can be used in the same way. The website provides access to publications and information and RSS feeds but the email alerting service is only available to those working in the public sector. Consultations are listed on Directgov with guidance on how the process works and how to respond.

White Papers

Once a government department has consulted on a topic and reached a view this will be published as a White Paper although, as we have seen above, this will not be how it is described on the title page. White Papers are normally Command Papers and as such will be laid before Parliament.

Press releases

Press releases are a useful source of information as they will have been carefully written to convey a department's view on a topic and should not be overlooked. They appear on departmental websites and through the alerting services and, of course, will be picked up and reported on by the media.

Advice and guidance

The Government publishes to inform, advise, guide and warn citizens. This may be to ensure that everyone is aware of their responsibility to pay taxes, to register to vote, to report deaths, births and marriages. It may be to advise people on ways to stay healthy and safe such as giving up smoking or driving safely. It may be to warn people of the consequences of breaking the law such as with drink-drive campaigns or speeding. It may be to convey detailed regulations for building, for fire prevention or for health and safety, or to communicate changes to legislation. All of this requires extensive published material, most of which you will now find available electronically, but this will be backed up with leaflets, other documents and media campaigns.

Reports

The citizens of the UK need to be able to hold the government to account and government departments will produce reports on their work to show progress made. An example from the Department for Communities and Local Government is the series of reports under the title *Form and Function: A Comparative Evaluation of the Effectiveness of Unitary Authorities and Two-tier Structures*. This looks at how unitary authorities perform compared to two-tier structures in local government and the series includes data and qualitative research. Annual reports were issued to show how a department had performed. Examples include *On the State of Public Health: Annual Report of the Chief Medical Officer 2009* published by the Department of Health and the *Intelligence and Security Committee's Annual Report for 2009–2010* published by the Cabinet Office. However, since 2010 departments are no longer required to publish these.

Gazettes

The *London*, *Edinburgh* and *Belfast Gazettes* are the UK's official newspapers of record. These are publications which have been produced for nearly 350 years and record events from an official perspective. You will find notices of insolvency, unclaimed Premium Bond numbers, buildings licensed to be used for marriages, Royal Proclamations such as changes to the design of coins and much more.

The Gazettes have been made freely available online and this includes free access to the archive, a fascinating source of information, not least for family history research. An RSS news feed means you can stay in touch with different types of notices without actually accessing the Gazettes, and the electronic publication is managed by TSO. The Gazettes are one of the public sector publications which are actively encouraging the reuse of their data and the information is available as pdfs and XML so that they can be easily reused. The information is covered by Crown Copyright and reuse needs to be licensed by *www.london-gazette.co.uk/reuse*.

For more information on reuse see the National Archives website section on information management *www. nationalarchives.gov.uk/informationmanagement*.

To read the Gazettes go to:

- London: *www.london-gazette.co.uk*
- Edinburgh: *www.edinburgh-gazette.co.uk*
- Belfast: *www.belfast-gazette.co.uk*

Key central government information resources

Central government websites

Government websites are now the key source of information about departmental publications, and departments rely on their websites to list and to disseminate their publications as well as provide access to information. In recent years the way this is done has greatly improved and you will find a link to 'publications' on many departmental sites and effective use of the medium to disseminate publications as well as other information. However, there is still a digital divide and for those who don't have access to the technology or the skills to access information online the social divide can become even greater.

In theory the electronic availability of government information can only be a good thing as it makes it accessible to a wider audience than print alone. However, there are issues to be addressed. The move to electronic publishing doesn't mean that everyone reads everything on a screen. In practice many documents need to be printed to be usable. The cost of this rests with the user, or it may be a library providing online access but unable to cover the cost of printing. Electronic-only also assumes access to the necessary technology and skills and, as discussed in Chapter 2, we are still a long way from universal access to both these requirements. For the socially and economically disadvantaged, being unable to access the information about, for instance, benefits will put them at an even greater disadvantage.

The government began using the web in 1995 but the initial aim was simply to load content and there was little concern about navigation, accessibility, usablility or archiving. This came later as the quantity of material grew and with the realisation that some content had disappeared or was simply untraceable. All the early sites had some shortcomings in coverage, indexing, navigation and accessibility, but in the years since they were first launched many lessons have been learned and the quality of the sites has improved greatly.

Many sites reflect the structure of central government, with each department creating its own departmental site and in many cases separate sites for specific areas of responsibility. In 2007–08 in response to a PQ the Department for Transport produced a list of websites for the department and its agencies which totalled 65. These included the main site for the Department for Transport *www.dft.gov.uk* but went on to list sites for specific areas of the department's work from separate agencies such as the Highways Agency to specific campaigns such as Cycle Smart and Arrive Alive. The list shows a spread of domains and naming conventions used.

Understandably sites have been established to support a particular topic or campaign. They may have been developed with catchy URLs that are easy to remember and indeed many have been very successful in promoting a particular issue. Examples include the Department for Transport site with the intriguing address of *www.hedgehogs.gov.uk*. This has now been put into hibernation and replaced by *www. talesoftheroad.direct.gov* but it still carries road safety games and competitions, although it no longer requires you to 'hog in'. 'Talk to Frank' at *www.talktofrank.com* provides advice on drugs and is part of a wider government campaign to combat drug abuse among young people.

Transformational Government: Enabled by Technology was published in 2005 as the first wave of e-government targets to develop online services and access to information were near to being met. It set out a strategy for a 'delivery of services designed around the needs of citizens and businesses' and it identified the need to rationalise government websites. By the time it published its first annual report in January 2007 a decision had been made to close 551 of the 951 government websites identified in an attempt to bring some order to the unimpeded growth of government on the web. The Coalition government conducted a further review of government websites and announced that the previous Government still had 794 in place by March 2010, although the newly elected Government claimed to have identified a total of 820 sites still in existence. Work continues to rationalise government on the web and to avoid duplication and mixed messages such as the Department of Health promoting healthy eating while the Potato Marketing Boards encourages us to love chips!

Part of the Transformational Government plan was for the Directgov site to be the focus for citizen information. Directgov is by the far the most successful of the attempts to bring together the information issued by the amorphous body which is central government and was originally developed in the wake of the UKonline programme. It has grown into what it aspired to be, which is the first port of call for information for citizens.

Examples

A number of government websites have been reviewed to give examples of the types of publications and information available, how they are presented and how easy it is to find what you need.

Department for Communities and Local Government

(*www.communities.gov.uk*)

The department is diverse and the website brings together information on a variety of topics. The home page is split into 'What we do' and 'News' and with a link to publications clearly visible. The site contains information about the structure and senior staff of the department and how it functions. It is used to make available the many different types of publications issued by the department.

These include consultations, circulars, impact assessments, corporate reports, legislation and policy, newsletters, manuals, leaflets and booklets, research and statistics. Each type can be searched by keyword and date or a search may be made of all publications. The publication scheme will tell you how long a series is held on the website. For instance, the Annual Report and Accounts is held for just two years. This is a very short period of time for this valuable information to be available, making comparisons of the department's performance over a period of time very limited. There is also information about ordering printed copies of the department's publications available on the site.

One example of a set of publications which are now provided on the website and which are updated as new ones are published is the Planning Policy Statements series. These 'explain statutory provisions and provide guidance to local authorities and others on planning policy and the operation of the planning system'. They can be found by following links to Planning and then Planning Policy and are listed in full. If you attempt to find these through the database of publications they are mixed up with other 'Good practice and guidance' publications which does not make locating them easy.

Statistics and Research are listed here and there is a detailed case study on the Communities and Local Government housing statistics site in Chapter 8.

Department for Business, Innovation and Skills (BIS)

(*www.bis.gov.uk*)

The Department for Business, Innovation and Skills (BIS) website has information about the governance of the department and details of the management board and team with biographies, its achievements, policies, partners and initiatives. BIS also has news on its home page and links to its major strategies as top-level links. It then has a link to 'Reports and Publications' which takes you to a database of publications with a free text search and the ability to search by the Unique Reference Number (URN) as well as a subject listing for browsing and an A–Z by title. There is a shopping basket facility for ordering publications, but documents are also offered as pdfs or as html files. Some material is only available in digital format.

Department of Energy and Climate Change

(*www.decc.gov.uk*)

As a comparison, and probably because it was established as recently as October 2008, this site has a short list of documents sorted by category with a pdf available for each. This works reasonably well with a list of publications covering the scope of the department and including all energy-related publications produced by the former Department for Business, Enterprise and Regulatory Reform. Earlier material has been archived by the National Archives as snapshots taken during 2008 and 2009.

HM Treasury

(*www.hm-treasury.gov.uk*)

The website for HM Treasury provides electronic access to the numerous documents associated with the Budget and pre-Budget Report, spending reviews and savings plans. It carries news and brings together consultations and relevant legislation. As with some other sites, the Treasury website carries transcripts of speeches made by the department's ministers. This is a useful source for checking the accuracy of what has been said. As with other sites, there is information about how the Treasury is organised, who are its ministers and senior civil servants, and how to make contact.

Non-ministerial departments

Technically, non-ministerial departments fit here but in many ways they have more in common with other public sector bodies which are covered in the next chapter. The websites for non-ministerial departments are also well established.

A good example is the Charity Commission (*www.charity-commission.gov.uk*). As the body responsible for registering and regulating charities in England and Wales, the Charity Commission collects huge quantities of information. It uses its website both to collect this information and to make it available to a wider audience. The site includes access to the register of charities for England and Wales, making it possible to search for details of any charity registered with the Commission. The result will show you the charity's financial performance and reporting record, objectives, history and trustees and any other charities with which the trustees are associated. The site also gives guidance for those operating a charity, how the Commission operates and allows charities to submit their returns online.

The Serious Fraud Office (*www.sfo.gov.uk*) offers advice to victims and witnesses of fraud and guidance on avoiding being a victim by providing information about the latest scams. You can access information about how the SFO works and view its reports and accounts.

Inquiries

There have been a number of situations where specific websites have been established to provide access to the information for a major inquiry.

The Hutton inquiry, the *Investigation into the Circumstances Surrounding the Death of Dr David Kelly* (*www.the-hutton-inquiry.org.uk*), is one example. Another high-profile example is the Shipman inquiry or the *Independent Public Inquiry into the Issues Arising from the Case of Harold Frederick Shipman* (*www.the-shipman-inquiry.org.uk*). Both inquiries collected large quantities of evidence and in the case of the Shipman inquiry there were six reports published as a result. Limited access to printed copies of the evidence and reports was criticised at the time but, it has to be said, the full records of proceedings and findings are still accessible. In the Shipman case, the number of victims means that online, electronic access makes it easier to locate details of individual cases than would be the case with printed copies.

Provided the sites are archived in such a way as to remain accessible this approach probably ensures better access, both now and in the future, to the evidence and findings of the inquiry than a traditional, print-only approach. The Chilcot Inquiry designed to 'identify lessons that can be learned from the Iraq conflict' has its own website at *www.iraqinquiry. org.uk*.

Bibliographic tools

Bibliographic tools in this sense are catalogues of official publications rather than software for managing bibliographies. They are essential to keep track of the publications of central government just as they are for any other category of publication. They provide the librarian and reader with standard sets of information about the publication and a structured way of viewing the published output of official bodies.

UKOP

(*www.ukop.co.uk*)

The United Kingdom Official Publications Database (UKOP) includes details of all Parliamentary and statutory publications (including acts and Statutory Instruments), as well as the publications of over 2,500 official bodies including central government departments, the devolved administrations, agencies and other bodies. It covers material back to 1980 and is a subscription service provided by TSO. It is web-based and of the 450,000 records on the system approaching 10 per cent now include either the full-text document within the database or a link to the document held on another website. The database is updated each weekday as documents are published or made available to TSO. At the time of writing the cost of a subscription is around £1,500.

UKOP covers the output of 2,500 official bodies but there are, as we saw at the very beginning of this book, many more bodies issuing information and publications. It is inevitable that a large, segmented organisation such as Parliament, central government, the devolved assemblies and other public bodies will have problems persuading everyone to stick to the rules when it comes to publishing. After privatisation in 1996 it was recognised that the risk of gaps in the bibliographic record was greater than before and in 2002 HMSO issued guidelines which were updated in 2005. All government departments and agencies are reminded of the importance of a comprehensive record of their published output and guidance is given on the steps which must be taken to ensure this happens. The guidance – *Maintaining the Bibliography of UK Official Publications* – is available on the National Archives website and sets out how government departments are required to deposit publications to ensure they are added to UKOP. It is to be hoped this leads to a good coverage but with a disparate pattern of publishing comprehensive coverage is unlikely to be achieved in practice.

British National Bibliography (BNB)

The *British National Bibliography* covers printed and electronic publications from 1950 for the UK and Republic of Ireland. BNB is a subscription service and can be supplied as a weekly printed publication or as a MARC Exchange File. Its emphasis is 'mainstream monographs available through normal book buying channels'. However, it is not particularly useful for tracing government and other official publications as it is selective in its coverage and it specifically points users to the catalogues produced by TSO for details of these publications.

The Stationery Office (TSO)

HMSO – or Her Majesty's Stationery Office – was first established in 1786 as part of HM Treasury and, as its name suggests, its role was the provision of stationery to government departments. It was set up in order to improve what were seen as expensive and inefficient processes in place at the time.

HMSO expanded into printing (mainly forms at that time) but by 1882 was the official publisher for both Houses of Parliament. Royal Letters Patent were granted by Queen Victoria in 1889 to formalise this role and the Controller of HMSO became 'printer to Her Majesty of all Acts of Parliament' and was also appointed to hold Crown copyright.

HMSO's role developed and it became the publisher of much of what was issued by government. In 1980 it became one of the first trading funds to be established. A trading bond can be set up where it can be shown that more than 50% of a department or executive agency's income is generated by trading. To begin with, it was protected in as much as departments were still required to use HMSO to manage their publications. From 1982 government departments were permitted to use other publishers and various agreements came into being. This included the Central Statistical Office (the pre-cursor of the Office for National Statistics) which worked with the Open University and the Health and Safety Executive which established its own publishing company, HSE Books.

In 1988 HMSO became an executive agency and in 1996 its trading functions were privatised. The Stationery Office (TSO), a private company, took on the publishing work but ultimate responsibility for the production of legislation, Command and House of Commons Papers and the official Gazettes and the management of Crown Copyright remained with HMSO. The Controller of HMSO remained the Queen's Printer of Acts of Parliament. This move led to more commercial publishers getting involved in official publishing and also departments managing the publication and distribution of their own material.

HMSO's role now is to put in place central contracts for publication of legislation, Command and Departmental House of Commons Papers and Official Gazettes, to provide advice and guidance to government departments on publishing and to ensure the bibliography of official publications is maintained.

In 2005 a new body was created in response to the reuse of public sector information legislation. The Office of Public Sector Information (OPSI) aimed to take a lead in releasing the hidden value of public sector information to the wider economy. HMSO firstly became part of OPSI and both bodies were attached to the Cabinet Office, and then in October 2006 OPSI with HMSO became part of the National Archives (*www.nationalarchives.gov.uk*). In 2008 responsibility for the Statute Law Database was also transferred to the National Archives.

This merger brings together the national archive for England, Wales and the central UK government with the development of policy for information management and official publishing.

TSO, as indicated above, is a private company and must compete for publication work alongside other companies. It has retained many of its publishing contracts and, perhaps most importantly, those with HMSO/OPSI for the publication of legislation and Command Papers etc. It currently still holds contracts with the Legal Services Commission for publication of the *Legal Services Commission Manual*, with the Medicines and Healthcare products Regulatory Agency (MHRA) for the *British Pharmacopoeia*, with HM Revenue and Customs for the *Integrated Tariff of the UK* and with the Qualifications and Curriculum Authority for all their priced and free publications.

Of course, what TSO are required to manage in many of these contracts today is not the relatively simple job of publishing a hard-copy book but publication in multi-formats and the associated complexity. It may be a hard-copy publication with CD or web content and may include email data feeds. Importantly there will be a need to review continually how the information is made available. TSO must keep pace with customer demand for better ways of accessing the information as improvements in technology become available.

As well as maintaining many contracts, TSO has lost others and this can make tracing official publications more difficult. A major example is Scottish Parliament publications which are now handled by R.R. Donnelley (formerly Astron), which won the contract in 2004 and use Blackwell's Bookshop in Edinburgh as their distributor. However, Crown Copyright material such as acts of the Scottish Parliament and Scottish Statutory Instruments are still published by TSO.

TSO's website *www.tso.co.uk* operates as any publisher's website giving access to details of all material published by TSO and includes the *Daily List* referred to below for tracking publications day by day. TSO also offers *TSO Select*, which is a standing order service based on categories of information. Libraries can sign up to receive all publications within a category, and advance payment is made calculated on the estimated output within the selected categories. This avoids the need to handle individual invoices for each publication.

Official Publications Online

In 2009 TSO introduced *Official Publications Online* (OPO) (*www.tsoshop.co.uk/officialpublicationsonline*) which provides an electronic alternative to *TSO Select*. Again categories may be selected but receipt of the documents is in pdf format which can be printed or downloaded for storage within an organisation's own systems. The main advantage of this system is the email alerts which form a valuable part of the service.

Some departments publish their own material while others will use TSO. At one time departments would publish catalogues of their publications but this no longer happens as the information about their publications is on the web.

Daily List

Published by TSO five times a week, the Daily List contains bibliographic details of publications issued by or made available by TSO, covering 'Parliamentary, Scottish Parliament, Official publications, Statutory Instruments, publications from Northern Ireland, Scotland and Agency titles'. It is freely available on the TSO website at *www. tsoshop.co.uk* and is also available as a subscription service, although now only electronically by email as production of the paper version ceased in 2009. It usefully highlights key publications, making it easier to see the publications most likely to receive media coverage or be requested by library users. The TSO Daily List cumulates to form the Weekly and Monthly List and then the Annual Catalogue.

TSO also issues an *Annual List of Statutory Publications* as a printed Supplement to the Gazettes and a *Monthly List of Statutory Publications* in the same way.

The Controller's Library dates back to the 1800s and although it is not complete it is believed to contain copies of the majority of titles published from then through to the present day. It is held by TSO and digitisation of its content is based on customer demand. Copies of publications can be supplied by TSO using this library as its source.

Case studies

It is probably easier to understand the role and importance of information from government departments by looking at some likely scenarios.

Looking for work

Problem: A young woman in her twenties finds herself out of work. She visits the website of the Department for Work and Pensions (DWP) (*www.dwp.gov.uk*) to see what help and advice they can offer her.

Solution: She looks at the information about the New Deal for over 25s. This provides help in getting back to work but she is keen to see what she can do to help herself first. There is a link to a job search which claims to list 400,000 jobs so she has a go and it steers her through narrowing her search down by the type of work, and various other aspects and then the geographical area in which she would like to work. Putting in her postcode, she turns up a number of possibilities and clicks on the entries to find out how to apply.

While she is looking for work what can she claim in the way of benefits? She finds the link to Job Seeker's Allowance which explains what the allowance is and who is eligible, and gives a phone number to call. However, this is during office hours only, but then she notices that she can apply online. This requires her to register with the Government Gateway, which she does, but she has to wait for an activation code which takes a couple of weeks to come before she can progress this application.

Information about the proposed route of a new high-speed rail link

Problem: The BBC News has carried a story about the announcement of the proposed route of a new high-speed rail link and a resident, who suspects they may live close to the route, wishes to find more information.

Solution: The BBC website carries a link to the website for the Department for Transport (*www.dft.gov.uk*). The resident finds that as this is a topical matter there is an easy-to-find link on the DfT website to the documents published about the rail line. These are extensive but have been set out in a logical way and can all be downloaded or printed. The quantity of information and documents is quite daunting and some of the plans take a long time to open. The resident decides that they need printed copies but the cost of printing what they need to see will be too great. There is information about ordering printed copies and eventually they find a note that copies have been deposited in local libraries.

Finding a college course

Problem: Parents moving to a new area are keen to check on the educational opportunities for their 16-year-old daughter who wants to following a career in hairdressing.

Solution: Using the Directgov website *www.direct.gov.uk* and the Directory of Central Government Departments they reach the website of the Department for Education (DfE). They find the EduBase database on the DfE website which should help them find suitable colleges, but struggle to understand the way it works. Eventually they discover that they are getting no results because they selected 'girls' in the gender field of the search – this would mean the educational establishment would take *only* girls and there are none of these in the area. The college details do not include details of the courses available or a link to the college's website so they return to Google to find this. However, the website of the DfE website does help them find the levels of achievement.

Returning to Directgov, however, they find a link to 'It's your choice: opportunities after 16'. Following the explanations of the choices on offer for this age group, they find a search of courses which can be done by subject and postcode and quickly find just what they are looking for.

References

Cabinet Office (2005) *Transformational Government: Enabled by Technology*, Cm 6683. London: TSO. Online at: *www.cio.gov.uk*.

Cabinet Office (2007) *Transformational Government: Our Progress in 2008 Technology*. Online at: *http://ctpr.org/wp-content/uploads/2011/03/tg08_part1.pdf*.

National Archives (2006, revised May 2010) *How to Publish a Command Paper*. A guide to what is a command paper and the procedures for printing, publishing and presentation to Parliament. Online at: *www.nationalarchives.gov.uk*.

6

Other public bodies including the National Health Service and the Police

This chapter covers:

- introduction;

- what is a public body?

- examples;

- publications and information;

- case studies.

Introduction

For most purposes and for the purposes of this book 'other public bodies' are treated as one category of public sector organisation. However, it is a large and diverse group. It includes the executive agencies, which themselves take a number of different forms, as well as non-departmental public bodies (NDPBs) and various other bodies such as the BBC and the Bank of England which are not easy to categorise. They exist to deal with many areas of life and, although some may have quite high profiles, there are equally many which we would struggle to name. There are advisory boards, committees, councils, groups and panels.

There are commissions, agencies, working groups, steering groups and units.

What is a public body?

The directory of public bodies published by the Cabinet Office defines a public body as one which is 'not part of a government department but carries out its function to a greater or lesser extent at arm's length from central government'. These public bodies are sponsored by government departments, and ministers are responsible to Parliament for their activities and for the appointment of members of the bodies. However, for the purposes of this book a wider definition is used and will include the public sector organisations included in Schedule 1 to the Freedom of Information Act but not covered in other chapters. Having said that, we will not be covering the bodies listed in Part IV, i.e. maintained Schools and other educational institutions, as their published output is not extensive and their role and functions are well understood. (It should be made clear that Schedule 1 does not list 100,000 bodies as such but identifies groups of organisations such as schools and GP practices which individually would add up to around 100,000 separate bodies encompassed by the FOIA.)

The organisations we are looking at here have functions which range across the whole gamut of government responsibilities from aviation to zoos. They include the British Library, Arts Council England, Sport England, the Homes and Communities Agency, the Qualifications and Curriculum Authority, the Low Pay Commission, the Committee on Standards in Public Life and many more. The Regional Development Agencies fit into this category of official body but are covered in Chapter 7 on local government.

'Quango' (quasi autonomous non-governmental organisation) is a term sometimes used in the context of public bodies. At one time the Cabinet Office website had a section dedicated to 'quangos' but then the term was no longer used officially although it is still used in the press. In fact, some of the bodies described as 'quangos' were actually non-departmental *government* bodies so to describe them as 'non-governmental' was confusing.

However, the Coalition government was quick to tackle this area after it was elected and it conducted a review of some 901 bodies, 679 of which were defined as quangos. Of these 192 were identified to be abolished of which 46 per cent are to be abolished completely, 17 per cent to be replaced by a committee or group, 16 per cent to have their responsibilities transferred to a government department, 13 per cent to another body and 4 per cent to become charities. This leaves 2 per cent for transfer to the private sector and another 2 per cent to local government, with 1 per cent still to be decided. The Public Bodies Bill will set out how these will be created, structured and disbanded in future.

Keeping track

Keeping track of public bodies can be difficult as they change and evolve. Not only are there major changes to contend with, as described above, but structural changes in government, and reports which recommend better structures for the delivery of services mean public bodies not infrequently are renamed and change their areas of responsibility.

The agencies that have cared for our countryside are a case in point. The National Parks Commission was established in 1949, and then, under the Countryside Act 1968 became the Countryside Commission. In 1999 it merged with the Rural

Development Commission to become the Countryside Agency. In 2006 the Countryside Agency merged with the Rural Development Service of the Department for Food and Rural Affairs and English Nature to become Natural England (*www.naturalengland.gov.uk*).

Keeping track of these changes is not easy. From the Cabinet Office list it would seem that the vast majority of listed public bodies have their own websites, but it varies as to whether they are part of the site of the parent department or have their own website. Some, but by no means all, are included on the Directgov website. Where they are listed there is usually a history of the body and a link to their website. Directgov is now seen as the core source for this type of information and, with the changes to quangos described above, carries the complete list of reviewed bodies (*Public Bodies Reform – Proposals for Change*).

Non-departmental public bodies (NDPBs)

Although separate from government departments, NDPBs carry out functions on behalf of the sponsoring departments which fund them and ensure they are effective. They are independent of the department, which enables them to make unbiased recommendations and decisions, and there are currently as many as a thousand. Until 2010 the Cabinet Office collated information about NDPBs and published the information in *Public Bodies*. Information on public bodies up to the end of 2009 can be found at *www.civilservice. gov.uk/ndpb*. It is not clear what will be published in future.

Public Bodies lists NDPBs by the department under which they sit and then the category into which they fit.

NDPBs fall into four categories as follows.

Executive NDPBs

Typically these are established in statute and carry out executive, administrative, regulatory and/or commercial functions. Examples include the Environment Agency for the Department for Environment, Food and Rural Affairs, the Homes and Communities Agency for the Department of Communities and Local Government, and Arts Council England, the British Library and the British Museum for the Department for Media, Culture and Sport.

Advisory NDPBs

Advisory NDPBs provide independent, expert advice to Ministers on a wide range of issues. Examples include the Advisory, Conciliation and Arbitration Service (ACAS) under the former Department for Business, Enterprise and Regulatory Reform, now the Department for Business, Innovation and Skills, and Cycling England for the Department for Transport.

Tribunal NDPBs

Tribunal NDPBs have jurisdiction in a specialised field of law. Examples include the Valuation Tribunal Service under the Department of Communities and Local Government.

Independent Monitoring Boards of Prisons, Immigration Removal Centres and Immigration Holding Rooms

These are independent 'watchdogs' of the prison system and were formerly known as Boards of Visitors (adapted from Cabinet Office, *Public Bodies 2009*). The number of such bodies has been reducing in recent years with 883 in 2006 down to 827 in 2007, 790 in 2008 and a further 42 removed by March 2009 when the list was last updated. There will have been new ones created in this time too and changes of names and areas of responsibility.

Scotland

Scotland, too, has a number of public bodies which contribute to the delivery of public sector services. A directory appears on the website *www.scotland.gov.uk/Topics/Government/public-bodies* and includes organisations such as the Cairngorms National Park Authority, the National Library of Scotland, the Police Complaints Commission and the Scottish Arts Council. The Scottish Government is responsible for:

- 33 executive NDPBs
- 46 advisory NDPBs (including 32 Justice of the Peace Advisory Committees)
- 38 tribunals (including 32 Children's Panels)
- 3 public corporations
- 23 NHS bodies.

There are also a number of other public bodies that operate in Scotland, which are the responsibility of Whitehall departments (part of the UK government) and these are included in the Cabinet Office publication referred to above.

Wales

Information about public bodies in Wales is a little more difficult to track down as the Cabinet Office list states there are none! However, the Welsh Assembly website gives details of how to apply to serve on one at: *wales.gov.uk/about/recruitment/publicapps/pubb/?lang=en*.

Here too are listed 18 Assembly Government sponsored bodies such as the Arts Council of Wales, the Brecon Beacons

National Park Authority, the Care Council for Wales, the Countryside Council for Wales, the Higher Education Funding Council for Wales, the National Library of Wales, the National Museum of Wales, the Pembrokeshire Coast National Park Authority, the Royal Commission on the Ancient and Historical Monuments of Wales, the Snowdonia National Park Authority, the Sports Council for Wales and the Welsh Language Board.

There are then five NHS bodies:

- community health councils
- local health boards
- National Health Service trusts
- National Advisory Board
- National Delivery Board.

Finally there is an extensive list of advisory bodies and other appointments which includes organisations such as:

- Ancient Monuments Advisory Board for Wales
- Child Poverty Expert Group
- Children's Commissioner for Wales
- Commissioner for Older People in Wales
- Economic Research Advisory Panel
- Fisheries, Ecology and Recreation Advisory
- Flood Risk Management Wales
- Fuel Poverty Advisory Group
- General Teaching Council for Wales.

Northern Ireland

Bodies sponsored by the Northern Ireland Executive were included in the Cabinet Office publication while there was no devolved government operational in Northern Ireland. Until 2007 a list of public bodies was published by the Public Service Improvement Unit of the Northern Ireland Department of Finance and Personnel at *www.dfpni.gov.uk*. Northern Ireland's Directgov website provides information for applying for an appointment but no list is published currently. See *http://www.nidirect.gov.uk/*.

Agencies

Some of the organisations which are non-departmental public bodies are known as agencies such as the Environment Agency. However, there are others which are referred to as agencies but which are non-ministerial departments. Examples of these are HM Land Registry and Ordnance Survey.

Executive agencies generally do not have their own legal identity but operate under delegated powers from ministers and departments. Some are trading funds such as Ordnance Survey and as such must generate income. Some are non-ministerial departments. They were formed as the result of the report commonly known as 'Next Steps' prepared by Sir Robin Ibbs in 1988 and were intended to focus on service delivery while the parent department concentrated on policy development. Executive agencies are included in the A–Z of Central Government on the Directgov website but not listed separately.

Regulatory bodies

Examples of public bodies

Probably the best way to try to understand the roles and functions and the publications and information of this body of organisations is to look at some examples of each category in more detail. Case studies have been included where appropriate to show what use might be made of the information available and how it can be accessed.

Executive NDPBs

Environment Agency

(*www.environment-agency.gov.uk*)

The Environment Agency is probably best known in recent years for its role in managing flooding and the well publicised 'Floodline'. However, the Agency is, of course, responsible for much more than just coping with flooding as its role is to protect the environment as a whole across England and Wales. In Scotland the same services are provided by the Scottish Environmental Protection Agency (*www.sepa. org.uk*). In Northern Ireland there is the Department of the Environment (*www.doeni.gov.uk*) and the Environment Agency (*www.ni-environment.gov.uk*) within that provides environmental protection services.

'Floodline' is an interesting example of where public demand for very specific information led to the development of an innovative and effective way of ensuring the right information reached the public as quickly as possible. Not only is the 'Floodline' able to offer information on request, but users can sign up to receive alerts to problems with a particular river by calling 0845 988 1188. The website was re-launched in 2008 to ensure all information, and in particular flood information, was easy to access. The flood maps can be searched by postcode, allowing property owners to see the level of risk of flooding for their location.

Health and Safety Executive (HSE)

(www.hse.gov.uk)

The Health and Safety Executive (HSE) is responsible for health and safety regulation in Great Britain and the HSE, working with local government, is also responsible for enforcement. The Department of Work and Pensions is the sponsoring department for the HSE and there are a range of advisory committees, boards and councils which advise them on particular hazards or particular sectors of industry. There are, for instance, advisory committees on dangerous substances, dangerous pathogens and toxic substances, a Construction Industry Advisory Committee, and committees concerned with health and safety in higher and further education, mining, printing, shipbuilding and small businesses. There are also advisory committees concerned with particular risks such as infectious diseases and asbestos.

HSE publications

The HSE publishes a comprehensive set of leaflets on a range of health and safety topics. Many are available on the website as pdfs but they can also be ordered online. Some of the leaflets are offered as MP3 files and called 'Talking leaflets'. They can be accessed via a computer using free software such as Windows Media Player or RealOne or can be stored to be listened to on a portable MP3 player. Other publications include research reports and operational guidance and a set of electronically available journals.

The HSE reports on its performance each year in its Annual Report and Accounts which is published as a Command Paper. It will also, like similar bodies, publish business plans and strategies to describe how it intends to improve the performance of the area for which it has responsibility.

Case study

Problem: A company health and safety officer responsible for ensuring the safety of staff whose jobs involve lifting and handling heavy loads has arranged training sessions but wants to be sure they have information to take away with them to remind them of what they have learned.

Solution: A visit to the HSE website at *www.hse.gov.uk* seems the obvious place to start, but it takes a little while to find the link under 'Resources' to 'HSE Books free to download or to buy' and a search brings up a selection of priced books and free leaflets. He opts for a free leaflet called *Getting to Grips with Manual Handling* but because he needs more than one he has to buy a pack of 10 at a minimal cost. He can request one free of charge so he does this to ensure it provides what he needs before ordering multiple copies. While he is visiting the site he sees that he can sign up to receive health and safety bulletins by email or RSS feed, but also via SMS text messaging. As he is often out and about, this seems the best way of keeping up to date with changes and it is free of charge. He decides it is worth a try because he can always unsubscribe if it gets to be too much and he should be up to speed on developments in health and safety.

Research councils

(*www.rcuk.ac.uk*)

Currently there are seven research councils in the UK:

- Arts and Humanities Research Council
- Biotechnology and Biological Sciences Research Council
- Engineering and Physical Sciences Research Council
- Economic and Social Research Council

- Medical Research Council
- Natural Environment Research Council
- Science and Technology Facilities Council.

Each was established under a Royal Charter, and statutory control for them rests with the Department for Business, Innovation, and Skills. Information about them and links to their individual websites are available on the Research Councils UK (RCUK) site *www.rcuk.ac.uk*.

Their role is to fund research using public sector money in the various specific areas they cover.

Sports councils

There are sports councils for each part of the UK which campaign to improve the provision of sports facilities and encourage the take-up of sport:

- Sport England (*www.sportengland.org.uk*)
- Sport Scotland (*www.sportscotland.org.uk/*)
- Sports Council for Wales (*www.sports-council-wales.org.uk/*)
- Sport Northern Ireland (*www.sportni.net/*).

The sports councils are required to publish annual reports and accounts, and they also undertake research, the results of which are published on their websites. Taking Sport England as an example, the website contains the results on work looking at, for instance, participation in sport, and has monitored the behaviour of different groups of people over a period of time to see how their involvement in sport has changed and the effectiveness of intervention activities in improving the take-up of sport.

Learning and Skills Council

(*www.lsc.gov.uk*)

The Learning and Skills Council was an NDPB and replaced the Further Education Funding Council and the Training and Enterprise Councils in 2001. It existed to improve the skills of people in England and was responsible for planning and funding education and training for all young people and adults not attending university. It was split into nine regional offices which match the local government regions. In Scotland the equivalent role is taken by the Enterprise Network and Futureskills Scotland.

The Learning and Skills Council gives us an example of the problems created by changes to the name, structure and responsibilities of public bodies. The website tells us the names of the bodies it replaced but can we find digital information about those organisations? The LSC was not established until 2001 so we would expect there to have been web content for the previous bodies. Thanks to the *Official Documents* site maintained by TSO, a Google search turns up a report from 1997 which describes the Further Education Funding Council as it was in 1997 (*www.archive.official-documents.co.uk*). This site covers Command Papers and other governmental publications in two sections covering 1994–2001 and 2002–05.

The government's White Paper, *Raising Expectations: Enabling the System to Deliver*, published in March 2008, recommended the closure of the LSC. Responsibility for education for 16–19 year olds has been transferred to local authorities and two new agencies established: the Young People's Learning Agency (*ypla.gov.uk*) (an NDPB of the Department for Children, Schools and Families) and the Skills Funding Agency (*skillsfundingagency.bis.gov.uk*) (part of the Department for Business, Innovation and Skills). The website at *www.lsc.gov.uk* has been closed and simply gives information and links to the new organisations.

Fortunately the LSC website was selected for inclusion in the UK Web Archive at *www.webarchive.org.uk* and a search of this site shows that it was last archived in January 2010.

Advisory, Conciliation and Arbitration Service (ACAS)

(*www.acas.gov.uk*)

ACAS was first established as a government service in 1896. It became the Industrial Relations Service in the1960s but in 1974 it was moved away from government, finally becoming the Advisory, Conciliation and Arbitration Service in 1975. It 'aims to improve organisations and working life through better employment relations' by 'providing up-to-date information, independent advice, high quality training' and 'working with employers and employees to solve problems and improve performance'.

ACAS is largely funded by the Department for Business, Innovation and Skills and is a non-departmental public body, priding itself on its impartial and independent status. ACAS publishes a set of information relating to employment issues. These include a set of free advisory leaflets on topics such as employing older workers, holidays and holiday pay, bullying, stress and Internet use at work.

There are also advisory handbooks on employment topics aimed at small businesses, research publications, codes of practice and a set of free factsheets on topics such as communication with employees and dealing with grievances. ACAS have also produced a training DVD for employment tribunals which gives advice on whether or not to take an issue to tribunal and, if a tribunal does take place, how to prepare for it and what to expect when you get there.

Case study

Problem: A small business has a member of staff who will shortly be 65 but does not want to retire. They are unsure of their legal position and want a quick and authoritative answer.

Solution: The ACAS website offers them a free leaflet *Employing Older Workers* and it is available as a pdf to download or as an html file or web page.

Agencies

Land Registry

(*www.landregisteronline.gov.uk*)

The Land Registry is the body responsible for registering title to land in England and Wales and recording dealings involving registered land such as sales or mortgages. It holds records for 19 million titles and these have been digitised so that they can be made available electronically. Access to the records is via Land Register Online at *www.landregisteronline. gov.uk* and information about land can be downloaded for a small fee paid by credit or debit card. Tracing the owner of a piece of land can be achieved this way by using the name of the property and the postcode or by using a map. The standard information available is a title plan and the title register which will provide you with the title number, the Land Registry office which deals with the title, the address of the land or property, the name and address of the owner or owners, the price for which it last changed hands and the mortgage lender if there is one.

The system makes what is personal data available to everyone with web access and a credit or debit card and it could at first glance seem to contravene the Data Protection Act. In fact the Land Register for England and

Wales has been open to the public since December 1999 and the Land Registration Act 2002, which came into effect from October 2003, extended the open register by making copies of mortgage deeds and leases available. The Land Registration Act and its associated rules (The Land Registration Rules 2003) require that this information is made publicly available. Section 34 of the Data Protection Act 1998 says that personal data is exempt if the 'data consists of information which the data controller, i.e. the Land Registry, is obliged by or under any enactment to make available to the public'.

However, not all records are available to download and you may be directed to print and submit a form if the details you require are not yet available electronically. A service for companies is available through Land Registry Direct at *www.landregistry.gov.uk*. This service enables users to set up a credit account and a user ID so that multiple searches can be undertaken and the costs accumulated – ideal for solicitors and lenders who need to access quantities of land registry data. At the time of writing there is a time limit on both services so that land registry information can only be purchased between 7 am and 12 noon Monday to Saturday.

Other information available through the Land Registry is the House Price Index which appears in brief on the home page, giving the average price and the monthly and annual change. A more in-depth search can be done for one location, or a comparison can be made using two postcodes with the results displayed as a graph and as a table.

Case study
Problem: A local authority constructing a new road needs to compulsorily purchase properties along the route and therefore needs to identify the owners.

Solution: Using the Land Registry service they are able to locate the properties by doing a search on the postcodes and are then able to download for a small fee a copy of the title plan and the title deed which gives the name and address of the owner. For a property where there is no postcode the area is located using the map on the site and as no online title deed is available a request for information is submitted via the site.

Companies House

(*www.companieshouse.gov.uk*)

While the Land Registry holds information about title to land, the equivalent for business information is Companies House. In a similar way to the Land Registry, Companies House has a duty to collect information for registration purposes which it then makes publicly available for a small charge. The Companies House website offers a service called WebCheck which allows anyone to search for companies and download the reports which they are required to deposit with Companies House as part of their registration. Charges, as with the Land Registry, are minimal with each report costing just £1 at the time of writing. The reports can be used to trace the directors of a company and to view their accounts so as to see whether it is a viable business.

Case study
Problem: A local authority which operates business units has received an application to let one of its units to a small local business. They want to ensure the company is registered and sound.

Solution: The Companies House website is used to find the basic information about the company, i.e. its registered address and category of business. Further information is then ordered to download. This includes the company's latest accounts and the current appointments. This provides the local authority with information which helps them in deciding whether or not the business is suitable as a tenant.

Highways Agency

(*www.highways.gov.uk*)

The Highways Agency is responsible for managing, maintaining and improving the motorways and trunk road network in England, leaving the local roads to be maintained by the appropriate local authority. In Scotland this responsibility rests with Transport Scotland, in Wales the Welsh Assembly, and in Northern Ireland the Roads Service which is an Agency within the Department for Regional Development.

As part of this role the Highways Agency is responsible for publishing the standards used for building and maintaining roads. These are numerous and include the *Design Manual for Roads and Bridges* (DMRB), the *Manual of Contract Documents for Highways Work* (MCDHW), *Traffic Advisory Leaflets* and *Traffic Signals Manual*.

The DMRB and MCDHW have been available electronically for some time which offers many advantages over the hard-copy volumes as this is an extensive loose-leaf publication, split into separate standards and updated quarterly. Many improvements have been made in recent years to the way these documents are published, including limiting updates to quarterly rather than publishing as and when a new or updated standard was issued which made it difficult to know if publications had been missed. These and many other standards are now published on the Highways Agency website *www.highways.gov.uk* under the headings 'Doing business with us' and 'Technical information'. Other publications produced by the Highways Agency include their annual report (as a House of Commons paper) and the findings of research and investigations.

To try to discover exactly what the Agency publishes from its website is not easy but for the persistent under 'About us' there is a list of links to corporate documents under headings such as 'Main Reports', 'Strategic Plans' and 'Partnership Documents' and a 31-page pdf list of publications with a publication code and title. These can be obtained from the Highways Agency publications distribution centre. Aside from publications the website carries information about road projects and traffic information which is provided through RSS feeds, e-mail alerts and widgets which can be used on social media pages or websites.

Meteorological Office (Met Office)

(*www.metoffice.gov.uk*)

Most of us use the services of the Met Office every day of our lives as we depend on the information it produces to know whether we need a coat, an umbrella or sun screen. The Met Office are expert at sharing information and, as well as the public face which we see and hear on the TV and radio throughout the day, they provide specialist services to airports and farmers.

Much of the information issued by the Met Office is not in the form of publications but weather reports, however they do produce a number of publications which include corporate reports etc., research and books on various weather-related topics as well as a set of subject guides and factsheets. The Met Office is responsible for operating the National Meteorological Library and Archive which offers free membership to everyone and an online catalogue, and is based in Exeter.

Regulatory bodies

In this category are included the bodies which have been established to regulate and promote aspects of our national life. These are numerous and include bodies such as the Health and Safety Executive (covered above in the section on agencies), the Audit Commission, the National Audit Office, the Equalities and Human Rights Commission, the Civil Aviation Authority and those responsible for industries such as Ofwat and Ofcom. The bodies change, develop and merge, and keeping track of these changes can be difficult.

A variety of publications are issued by regulatory bodies which include annual reports, performance reporting, policy documents, press releases, consultations, licensing information and guidance on how things can be improved.

Examples

Audit Commission

(*www.audit-commission.gov.uk*)

The role of the Audit Commission is one of scrutiny. It was established under the Audit Commission Act 1998 to be an independent public body with a remit to ensure public money is used economically, effectively and efficiently. It is responsible for the assessment of 11,000 public bodies in England. The most prolific of its publications is the series of reports prepared on local authorities as a result of inspections. These can be used, for instance, to give local people information about the performance of their local authority. The Coalition government have announced plans to disband the Audit Commission and it is anticipated that inspection of local government will be managed in different ways after 2012.

Ofwat

(www.ofwat.gov.uk)

Ofwat or the Water Services Regulation Authority is the regulatory body for the water and sewerage services in England and Wales. It provides information about the industry and how it functions, including giving details of the water companies and their ownership, advice for householders and other water users, and information on the prices set for the industry. There is a link to publications from the home page of the website and these are arranged by date, subject and categories such as reports, consultations, media briefings and leaflets. You will find on this website the contact details for all the water companies operating and information about mergers and acquisitions.

The National Audit Office

(www.nao.org.uk)

The National Audit Office describes its mission as 'helping the nation spend wisely'. It is responsible for auditing public sector accounts and aims to help the government achieve value for money. Because much of its work results in published reports, its website features the latest of these on its home page and the link to publications appears as the first link and is then split up by work in progress and by sector. An archive from 1984 to 1998 is included which is useful. The featured reports have an abstract of the report and publication details, and are available as a pdf and with links to related information. They are published as House of Commons Papers and are numbered accordingly, i.e. a sequential number and the session years, e.g. HC 529 Session 2006–07.

The Care Quality Commission

(www.cqc.org.uk)

The Care Quality Commission was established in March 2009 and replaced the Healthcare Commission, the Commission for Social Care Inspection and the Mental Health Act Commission. It is the regulator for health and social care in England. Publications from the previous bodies are available from the website of the new body. See the section below on the Police for information about Her Majesty's Inspectorate of Constabulary and see above for details of the Audit Commission (discussed further in the section on 'Performance and inspection information' in Chapter 7).

Her Majesty's Courts and Tribunal Services

Tribunals

Tribunals are a major and rather different category of public sector body in as much as they exist to adjudicate between government and the public in various areas such as employment, social security, asylum, etc. and therefore have a quasi-judicial role. A review of how they were working was undertaken by Sir Andrew Leggett and his recommendations were picked up in the Tribunals, Courts and Enforcement Act 2007. The Tribunals Service created in 2006 was an executive agency of the Ministry of Justice (MoJ) and provided administrative support to the tribunals' judiciary. On 1 April 2011 the Tribunal Service merged with Her Majesty's Court Service to form HM Courts and Tribunal Service. The website sets out the role of the service as being 'responsible for the administration of the criminal, civil and family courts and tribunals in England and Wales and non-devolved tribunals in Scotland and Northern Ireland. It provides for a fair, efficient and effective justice system delivered by an independent judiciary'.

As a result of the 2007 Act a First-Tier Tribunal was established which consists of six chambers and these still operate within the new organisation:

- General Regulatory Chamber, covering (among other topics) charity, consumer rights, environment, information rights
- Health, Education and Social Care Chamber
- Immigration and Asylum Chamber
- Social Entitlement Chamber
- Tax Chamber
- War Pensions and Armed Forces Compensation Chamber.

There is then an Upper Tribunal which is the court of record and hears appeals, certain other cases, judicial reviews and enforcement.

Tribunals handle large numbers of cases with, for instance, the Employment Tribunal accepting 236,100 claims in 2009–10, a 56 per cent increase on the previous year. Of these 95,200 were claims related to the working time directive, 75,500 for unauthorised deductions and 57,400 for unfair dismissal.

The Tribunal Service published annual reports, business plans and statistics, and these have been archived by the National Archives with a link on the HM Courts and Tribunals Service website. It is assumed that it will continue to publish similar information as part of the new body.

The National Health Service

Introduction

The National Health Service (NHS) is a vast public body producing huge quantities of material which, as in local government, stretch from the strategic to the mundane.

Structure and functions

The NHS was established in 1948 as a result of the Beveridge Report presented to Parliament in 1942. The structure of the NHS changes frequently but essentially for operational service delivery in England the NHS is split into primary and secondary care.

Primary care includes GPs, dentists, opticians, pharmacists, the NHS Direct service and the NHS Walk-in Centres.

Secondary care covers emergency and urgent care, ambulance trusts, NHS trusts which provide hospital services, mental health trusts and care trusts.

Funding, direction and support for the NHS are provided by the Department of Health. There are currently 10 strategic health authorities (SHAs) whose role is to develop plans for the provision of health care within their areas and to scrutinise the various trusts which provide health services at a local level. Twenty-eight SHAs were first introduced in 2002 but the number was reduced to 10 in 2006, with plans announced in 2010 by the Coalition government to phase them out. The aim is to establish Public Health England as the primary care trusts and strategic health authorities are dissolved, and then create an NHS Commissioning Board which will provide funding to GPs and GP commissioning consortia.

Currently trusts exist to provide services at a local level.

- *Acute trusts* manage hospital provision for an area although some 67 are now foundation trusts.

- *Foundation trusts*, introduced in 2004, have greater financial and operational freedom and the intention is that they match provision more closely to local needs.

- *Ambulance trusts* manage the provision of emergency and some non-emergency transport of patients.

- *Care trusts* are few in number as yet but where they exist they link the NHS and the local authority in providing health and social care and may also provide mental health services or primary care services.

- *Mental health trusts* are responsible for the provision of health and social care to those with mental illness.

- *Primary care trusts* (PCTs) manage the provision of GP surgeries, dentists, opticians and pharmaceutical services. PCTs will be replaced by GP consortia by April 2013.

Added to the above NHS bodies are the special health authorities set up to manage a particular aspect of health care across the UK. The number of these was reduced in 2006 to just 13 as listed below:

- *Health Protection Agency* – 'to protect the community (or any part of the community) against infectious diseases and other dangers to health' (HPA Act 2004) (*www.hpa.org.uk*).

- *Mental Health Act Commission* – 'safeguarding the interests of all people detained under the Mental Health Act' (*www.mhac.org.uk*).

- *National Institute for Health and Clinical Excellence* – 'responsible for providing national guidance on promoting good health and preventing and treating ill health' (*www. nice.org.uk*).

- *National Patient Safety Agency* – 'to identify issues relating to patient safety and to find appropriate solutions' (*www. npsa.nhs.uk*).

- *National Treatment Agency* – 'to improve the availability, capacity and effectiveness of treatment for drug misuse in England' (*www.nta.nhs.uk*).

- *NHS Appointments Commission* (*www.appointments.org. uk/index.htm*).

- *NHS Blood and Transplant* – 'to provide a reliable, efficient supply of blood, organs and associated services to the NHS' (*www.nhsbt.nhs.uk*).

- *NHS Business Services Authority* – 'the main processing facility and centre of excellence for payment, reimbursement, remuneration and reconciliation for NHS dental practitioners, pharmacists, NHS pensioners and other affiliated parties' (*www.nhsbsa.nhs.uk*).

- *NHS Direct* – 'to provide information and advice about health, illness and health services, to enable patients to make decisions about their healthcare and that of their families' (*www.nhsdirect.nhs.uk*).

- *NHS Litigation Authority* – 'responsible for handling negligence claims made against NHS bodies in England, family health services appeals and equal pay claims' (*www. nhsla.com*).

- *The Health and Social Care Information Centre* – 'collects, analyses and distributes national statistics on health and social care' (*www.ic.nhs.uk*).

- *The NHS Institute for Innovation and Improvement* – 'supports the NHS to transform healthcare for patients and the public by rapidly developing and spreading new ways of working, new technology and world-class leadership' (*www.institute.nhs.uk*).

- *NHS Professionals* – 'to provide high-quality flexible staff to Acute, Primary Care and Mental Health organisations across England' (*www.nhsprofessionals.nhs.uk*).

Publications and information

The NHS has been very successful in drawing together its information onto one set of clearly branded web pages at *www.nhs.uk*. The pages provide access to health advice and medical information. They are interactive, asking for feedback and offering online quizzes and calculators, and they give access to the 'Map of Medicine' developed as a diagnostic tool which provides flow charts for the identification and treatment of medical conditions.

The pages now include the information required for patients to 'choose and book' in line with the government's commitment to offer patient choice. Patient choice was set out as a policy in 2003 in *Building on the Best: Choice, Responsiveness and Equity in the NHS* (Cm 6079). The choice now being offered to patients means that it is essential that information is available to support those choices such as hospital facilities and clinical quality. Booking is also an option via the website, making it possible for someone who has been referred by a GP for treatment for a particular condition to search by the condition and then by postcode, to identify the hospitals where that treatment is offered. They will then be able to see how well the hospitals score on waiting times, whether or not an overnight stay is necessary, how often that hospital trust performs this operation or procedure, their MRSA infection rates, the Health Commission rating for the overall quality of service and a number of other measures of patient satisfaction. For those without Internet access the provision of the information required to help make the necessary choices will need to be facilitated by a member of NHS staff.

There is no link to publications on the NHS website but it is a good example of a site where the focus is on the provision of information in a way which suits the medium.

The main NHS website (*www.nhs.uk*) provides health and medical information, and information about the organisation, its history, structure and services. The NHS has a clear design to its website and it is easy to navigate and recognise.

It seems that you can move easily from information about health to information about obtaining treatment and the choices on offer. Individual hospital information is available from the NHS website, but hospitals also manage their own sites with more detailed information for patients and visitors, especially where foundation trust status has been achieved and the hospital is accountable to the community. Similarly, the individual bodies responsible for specific services within the health service also operate separate websites. An example is the Health Protection Agency whose responsibility is to protect the community against infectious diseases or any other dangers to health. They are the body that deals with chemical and radiation hazards and will be called in if there is an incident which puts the public at risk such as a fire with asbestos involved, a chemical spill or the outbreak of infectious diseases such as seasonal influenza. Their website carries useful guidance for the public and health professionals including data on topics such as levels of infection for 'flu and the take-up of vaccinations.

Northern Ireland

The NHS in Northern Ireland is made up of one Health and Social Care Board (HSCB) whose role is to commission services (*www.hscboard.hscni.net*) with five Local Commissioning Groups and five Health and Social Care Trusts for different geographical areas of the country. Alongside the Board are the Northern Ireland Ambulance Services HSC Trust.

- Public Health Agency: *www.publichealth.hscni.net*
- Business Services Organisation: *www.hscbusiness.hscni. net* and
- Patient and Client Council: *www.patientclientcouncil. hscni.net*

The website *www.n-i.nhs.uk* is described as a 'gateway' and includes information about health care provision as well as social care, covering areas such as fostering and social services as these are all delivered by these agencies rather than by local authorities.

Scotland

Health in Scotland is the responsibility of the Scottish Government and information about the structure is therefore on the Scottish Government website at *www.scotland.gov.uk*.

Fourteen NHS Boards plan, commission and deliver health services, and seven Special NHS Boards provide services across the country such as ambulance services and NHS 24 (*www.nhs24.com*) which provides health information and self-care advice by phone and via the Internet.

There is information on *Scotland's Health on the Web* at *www.show.scot.nhs.uk/* and the site explains that this is a portal site bringing together information about the many organisations in Scotland involved in the provision of health services. This is a useful approach and although it contains health information it is a website for the professional rather than the patient.

Wales

In Wales as in Scotland responsibility for health services is a devolved responsibility which rests with the Health and Social Care Department of the Welsh Assembly Government. Information about health issues, publications and research is available on the Welsh Assembly Government website *www.wales.gov.uk* – select the link to Health and Social Care.

The Health Commission Wales is responsible for services which are better delivered at a regional or national level such as blood and screening services and the NHS Direct Wales service which offers advice over the phone or through an online inquiry form (*www.nhsdirect.wales.nhs.uk*).

Information about health provision in Wales is offered through *www.wales.nhs.uk* which includes the Health of Wales Information Service (HOWIS). HOWIS provides an NHS Directory giving contact details for accident and emergency and other hospitals, GP surgeries, pharmacies, dental practices, opticians, NHS trusts, local health boards, community health councils and other national programmes and services. There is also information on jobs and careers in the NHS Wales, Public Health, the Health Watchdog which offers independent and confidential advice in dealing with problems with the NHS, and Health Statistics Publications. There is a link here too for NHS staff to the NHS Wales e-library for health where they can access free or licensed information resources. Similar services are provided in Scotland where it is known as the Knowledge Network (*www.elib.scot.nhs.uk*) and in England where it was known as the National Library of Health but is now called Health Information Resources (*www.library.nhs.uk*).

Police

The Home Office is responsible for policing in England and Wales and the Scottish Executive is responsible for policing in Scotland. As we have seen, responsibility for policing in Northern Ireland has been transferred to the Northern Ireland Assembly. Policing in the UK is carried out by 43 separate forces each with responsibility for a geographical area.

As well as these there are specialist forces:

- *British Transport Police* – providing police services for the railways (*www.btp.police.uk*).

- *Central Motorway Policing Group* – providing policing of the Midlands motorway network south from Cheshire on the M6 to the Welsh borders on the M50 and covering the police areas of the West Midlands, West Mercia and Staffordshire (*www.west-midlands.police.uk/cmpg*).

- *Civil Nuclear Constabulary* (CNC) (formerly UKAEA Constabulary) – providing policing for civil nuclear licensed sites and safeguarding nuclear materials, nuclear site operators, etc. (*www.cnc.police.uk*). The CNC reports to the Civil Nuclear Police Authority (*www.cnpa.police.uk*).

- *Ministry of Defence Police* (*www.mod.uk*).

- *Port of Dover Police* (*www.doverport.co.uk*).

- *Port of Liverpool Police* (*www.portofliverpool.police.uk*).

- *The Serious Organised Crime Agency* (SOCA) (*www.soca.gov.uk*).

- *Scottish Drug Enforcement Agency* (*www.sdea.police.uk*).

In each area of England and Wales there is an independent Police Authority made up of local people whose role is to ensure the police force for the area is effective and efficient. Each Police Authority is usually made up of 17 people, although some metropolitan areas have 19 members. There will be nine local councillors, three local magistrates and five independent people. The body which brings all of these together is the Association of Police Authorities (*www.apa. police.uk*).

Her Majesty's Inspectorate of Constabulary (HMIC) *www.hmic.gov.uk* is an independent body responsible for inspecting and recommending improvements to the Police service in England, Wales and Northern Ireland. It reports to the Home Secretary through Her Majesty's Chief Inspector of Constabularies. In Scotland there is a separate inspectorate, HM Inspectorate of Constabulary for Scotland.

The National Policing Improvement Agency (*www.npia. police.uk*) was formed as a result of the Police Reform White Paper *Building Communities, Beating Crime* published in 2004 and brought into being by the Police and Justice Act 2006. It is an NDPB and it combined the pre-existing organisations, the Police Information Technology Organisation (PITO) and the training body CENTREX. Its objective is to 'support the police service by providing expertise in areas as diverse as information and communications technology, support to information and intelligence sharing, core police processes, managing change and recruiting, developing and deploying people'. Its website carries details of research and training, its governance and initiatives. It publishes an annual report and a monthly Digest which aims to keep police informed of changes in legislation and key issues relevant to their areas of work. Because its role is to support the police, the content of the website is aimed at police staff and officers and includes details of courses and projects.

Publications and information

The websites for the 43 local police forces carry information about the local force, contact details, news and initiatives to reduce crime.

An attempt has been made to bring police information together and make it accessible to the public so as to reduce the number of non-emergency calls made to the police. *Ask the Police* at *www.askthe.police.uk* is operated by the Police

National Legal Database and uses the information held in the database to answer frequently asked questions.

The Home Office provides a section of its website which is dedicated to policing information and is aimed at 'serving police officers and anyone involved in policing and justice' (*www.police.homeoffice.gov.uk*). This includes organisational information such as human resources policies and guidance, the approach to equalities and diversity, business planning and finance, and information on specific areas of policing such as community policing, road traffic work and details of the National Policing Plan.

Her Majesty's Inspectorate of Constabulary (*www.inspectorates.homeoffice.gov.uk/hmic*), as the regulatory body for the police, publishes an assessment of the performance of the 43 police forces allowing comparison across the country. It also publishes business plans which were known as annual reports until 2007.

References

Department for Communities and Local Government (2009) *Establishment of Leaders' Boards: Guidance on the Preparation of Schemes.*

Department for Transport, Local Government and the Regions (2002) *Your Region, Your Choice: Revitalising the English Regions.* Archived at: *www.communities.gov.uk*

Department of Health (2003) *Building on the Best: Choice, Responsiveness and Equity in the NHS.* London: TSO Online at: *www.dh.gov.uk*

HM Treasury, Department for Business, Enterprise and Regulatory Reform and Department for Communities and Local Government (2007) *Review of Sub-national Economic Development and Regeneration.* Online at: *www.*

hm-treasury.gov.uk/sub-national_economic_development_regeneration_review.htm

Home Office (2004) *Building Communities Beating Crime. A Better Police Service for the 21st Century,* Cm 6360. London: TSO.

Ibbs, Sir Robin (1988) *Improving Management in Government: The Next Steps.* London: HMSO.

Office of the Deputy Prime Minister (2003) *Sustainable Communities: Building for the Future.* Online at: *www. communities.gov.uk.*

7

Local government including the Fire Service

This chapter covers:

- structure of local government;
- responsibilities of different types of local authorities;
- the way local authorities function;
- publications and information;
- the Fire Service;
- finding local authority information;
- further reading;
- case studies;
- information for local government.

Introduction

Local authorities issue information on a wide range of topics from abandoned vehicles to childcare, from climate change to planning and from rubbish collection to weddings. Every function of a local authority spawns information and in England and Wales alone there are 410 local authorities employing over 2.1 million staff, spending in the region of £70bn a year (25 per cent of public spending) and with a total of some 21,000 elected members (figures from the Local Government Association (LGA) *www.lga.gov.uk*).

Much of what is published is of an ephemeral nature and will be in the form of leaflets or web content with little apparent long-term value. While it is current, however, this material has an important role in society as it conveys to the citizen the information they need in order to access the public services provided by local councils. Many of these services are essential to the social, economic and environmental well-being of residents and include education, social care and maintenance of the highway network. If it survives, this information can also provide rich material for social historians.

Local authorities have a statutory requirement to make available more formal publications such as policy and strategy documents and the public record of the authority's decision-making process as contained in the agenda and minutes of council and committee meetings.

Structure of local government

Many of the entities which make up local government as it is today have their roots deep in history. The Shires south of the Tees, for instance, are referred to in the Domesday Book, while the Local Government Act 1888 created 62 elected county councils including the London County Council and 61 county borough councils in England and Wales. Legislation in 1894 revived the parishes and created urban district, rural district and non-county boroughs.

Currently, in some areas there are two tiers of local government with boroughs or districts and then county councils, and responsibility for services is shared between them. In other areas unitary authorities have been created with responsibility for all services. Scotland and Wales established unitary authorities in all areas in 1996 and the London boroughs are unitary authorities.

In 1996, 13 unitary authorities were created in England to replace the counties of Avon, Cleveland, Humberside and York City. In 1997 and 1998 a further 32 unitary authorities were created. Further unitary authorities were created in 2009 with Bedfordshire County Council and its three districts and boroughs replaced by two unitary authorities, Cheshire County and its six second-tier authorities becoming Cheshire East and Cheshire West. Cornwall, Durham, Northumberland, Shropshire and Wiltshire all became unitary authorities with a single authority replacing the county and district councils for the areas. However, the change of government in May 2010 brought a rethink of the unitary plans for Exeter, Suffolk and Norwich and these were quickly shelved.

In many of the two-tier areas there are also town or parish councils with limited powers and responsibilities but there are around 10,000 of them!

The structure of local government can be confusing as the pattern is not the same across the UK and it seems unlikely it ever will be. This means that it is sometimes difficult to identify which level of local government is responsible for which services. The current model of local government was established in the main in 1974 (Local Government Act 1972) but there were further changes in the 1990s (Local Government Act 1992) and the debate continues as to the most suitable model.

In October 2006 a White Paper on the future of local government was published but the changes which emerged from this were not extensive. The creation of the nine unitary authorities described above came out of this, while others chose to work to deliver services through 'enhanced two-tier working' (*Strong and Prosperous Communities – the Local Government White Paper 2006*, Department of Communities and Local Government).

The Local Government and Public Health Act 2007 brought into force the recommendations of the White Paper and provided for a strengthened role for councillors, stronger local partnerships, a wider and stronger role for scrutiny and changes to inspections and to parish councils.

Responsibilities of the different types of local authorities

The two-tier model – counties with districts or boroughs

In areas where there is a county council and then districts or boroughs the county council takes responsibility for

- countryside recreation
- education
- fire services
- highways
- libraries
- passenger transport
- rights of way and footpaths
- social services
- strategic planning
- transport planning
- waste management.

The district or borough councils within the area will provide

- environmental health
- housing
- local planning

- leisure and recreation
- licensing
- waste collection.

The district or borough council will also be responsible for collecting council tax from residents for itself and on behalf of the county and, where they exist, for parish or town councils.

Unitary authorities

Unitary authorities take responsibility for all locally provided public services. This will include education, housing, planning, strategic planning, transport planning, passenger transport, highways, fire, social services, leisure and recreation, libraries, waste collection, waste disposal and environmental health. They will also be responsible for collecting council tax to pay for these services.

Parish councils

Where parish councils exist they have very limited responsibilities but they have the advantage of being very locally focused and can ensure an area is well maintained. This may be by either doing things themselves or by lobbying for action by the district or county councils. Parishes will often have recreation grounds to maintain, may provide village halls and may administer allotments and cemeteries. They are consulted on planning matters and other issues by the districts or boroughs, unitary authorities or county councils. The Local Government White Paper published in October 2006 recommended a greater role for this tier of local government and the lifting of barriers to creating parish councils. District or unitary authorities and the London boroughs are able to create parish councils and decide what they are to be called. New parishes have been created as a result of the Local Government and Public Involvement in Health Act 2007 and examples include four in the St Austell area of Cornwall which were formed on 1 April 2009 and are the St Austell Town Council, Carlyon Parish Council, St Austell Bay Parish Council and Pentewan Valley Parish Council.

A Quality Parish Councils initiative was launched in 2003 and updated in 2008 by which time 357 parish and town councils had achieved quality status. Apart from showing they meet certain criteria, this status makes little difference to a parish or town council's operations or to its responsibilities. It is anticipated, however, that quality status will put town and parish councils in a better position to take on further responsibilities as outlined in the Local Government White Paper of 2006 and by the Coalition government, including the setting and enforcing of bye-laws.

Parish meetings

In the very smallest parishes with fewer than 150 electors there is a further form of local government. These are called a 'parish meeting'. These should not be confused with the annual parish meeting which all parish and town councils are required to hold and which are an opportunity for the electorate to hear about the work of their parish or town council. Where there is a parish meeting all the electors in the parish can take part and a chairman and clerk are elected and become legally responsible for all the decisions made by the parish meeting.

Town councils

Town councils have identical responsibilities to parish councils, the only difference between the two being that town councils can appoint a mayor and parishes have a chairman.

Charter trustees

In towns or cities where borough councils disappeared under the Local Government Act 1972 and where local people were reluctant to lose their mayor, a group known as Charter Trustees could be established. The Charter Trustees Order 1974 provided for these to be created and they exist in places such as Bath, Margate and Weston-super-Mare. In other areas, for instance Royal Leamington Spa, they were established in 1974 but then dissolved and replaced by town councils.

Localism

The Coalition government which came to power in May 2010 continues to support an enhanced role for parishes and has tabled a Localism Bill which, if it becomes law, will give local communities more power over areas such as housing and planning. The Explanatory Notes for the Bill say that:

> A key element of the Bill is to provide for community empowerment with powers to enable people to instigate local referendums on any issue, to approve or veto in a referendum a council tax increase deemed to be excessive, to express an interest in running local authority services and to provide local community groups with an opportunity to bid to buy assets of community value.

This legislation would also pave the way for directly elected mayors and would reform the planning system through the abolition of regional strategies, the provision of neighbourhood plans, compulsory pre-application consultation and changes to planning enforcement, and would bring about change in the way planning permission is managed for nationally significant infrastructure.

Metropolitan boroughs

Metropolitan boroughs (also known as metropolitan districts or authorities) have similar responsibilities to unitary authorities except that separate joint bodies exist to provide passenger transport, and fire and civil defence. They were formed in 1974 but at that time there were metropolitan counties and the boroughs acted as second-tier authorities to them. The metropolitan county councils were abolished in 1985 and the boroughs or districts became unitary authorities. Some have been granted city status, e.g. Coventry City Council (*www.coventry.gov.uk*). Examples of metropolitan authorities are Solihull Metropolitan Borough Council (*www.solihull.gov.uk*) and Wirral Metropolitan Borough Council (*www.wirral.gov.uk*).

London

London consists of 33 London boroughs which are all unitary authorities and the Greater London Authority (GLA) which was established in 2000 with an elected mayor. The GLA is responsible for setting strategies for London and is described in Chapter 7 'Regional Government'. The London boroughs are unitary authorities and as such have responsibility for the full range of public services.

Scotland

Scotland has 32 unitary authorities as well as about 1,200 community councils. The latter must be consulted by the unitaries on issues such as planning and development but are not entitled to set a precept. All areas of Scotland have community council areas identified, but community councils only exist and function if volunteers are available to take action.

Wales

Wales has 22 unitary authorities. Community councils exist in Wales too and, as in Scotland, all areas are designated as community council areas. Unlike Scotland, however, the community councils of Wales can raise a precept (i.e. council tax) and their powers are identical to those of the English parish councils. They can decide to call themselves town councils and can apply to the Crown for permission to be known as a city.

Community or parish meetings

Community meetings are held in Wales and, as with the Parish Meetings in England, are open to all the electors of a community or a parish. These are held in areas which are too small to support a community or parish council of their own.

Northern Ireland

Local government in Northern Ireland is slightly different to the remainder of the UK in that some of the functions normally associated with local government are delivered by central government or government agencies. There are 26 local councils in Northern Ireland and their responsibilities include:

- refuse collection and disposal
- environmental health
- building control
- parks and open spaces
- economic development
- leisure and amenities
- environmental protection.

Areas managed by central government are:

- education
- personal social services
- roads
- public housing
- the fire service
- the police
- trading standards
- drainage water
- sewerage
- libraries
- planning
- street lighting
- the collection of rates
- transport.

For more information see the Northern Ireland Local Government Association at *www.nilga.org/home.asp*.

Isle of Man, Jersey and Guernsey

The Isle of Man and the Channel Island bailiwicks of Jersey and Guernsey are Crown Dependencies. In other words they are possessions of the British Crown. They are not part of the United Kingdom but belong to what is known as the British Islands. They do not send representatives to the UK Parliament and they are not members of the European Union and, of course, they have their own Parliaments. They are included here because they do have a local government structure.

The Isle of Man is made up of 24 local authorities:

- 4 town authorities

- 2 district authorities

- 3 village authorities and

- 15 parish authorities.

Some of these authorities have websites but there is considerable variation in the scale and content. They can be accessed through the Isle of Man's government website at *www.gov.im* and the Department of Local Government and the Environment site *www.gov.im/dlge* has information about the structure and functions of local authorities on the Isle of Man.

Jersey has a local government based on parishes of which there are 12 (*www.parish.gov.je*). Meetings of the Parish Assembly are held as required and at these all registered electors may vote.

Guernsey similarly has ten parishes. Members are known as Douzenier and the Executive Officers who carry out the day-to-day administration of the parish are known as Constables (*www.gov.gg*).

The way local authorities function

The internal structure of local authorities and the way in which they function was the focus of the government's modernising local government agenda set out in a White Paper *Modern Local Government: In Touch with the People* issued in 1998 by the then Department of Transport, Local Government and the Regions. The intention was to modernise the way local government made decisions and to give local people a choice about the way their own authority functioned. The resulting legislation, the Local Government Act 2000, specified three possible models for the executive. It could consist of :

- an elected mayor who appoints two or more councillors to form the executive;
- an executive leader elected by the full council, plus two or more councillors appointed by the leader or the council; or
- a directly elected mayor with an officer of the authority appointed by the council as council manager.

Section 21 of the Act provides for overview and scrutiny committees which review or scrutinise decisions made by the executive. Each of these models is in use although there are currently only 11 directly elected mayors.

Local government publications

With so many separate authorities producing information and publications, the task of finding and exploiting this vast resource can be challenging.

Ideally the customer or citizen should not need to understand the structure of local government in order to access the information or the services they require. In fact, neither should you really need to know whether the service you wish to access is provided by central or local government.

In practice, to trace local authority publications and information does require a level of understanding of how local government is organised and how this fits into the wider picture. Hence the need to explain this at the beginning of this chapter.

The development of the Directgov website at *www. directgov.gov.uk*, which aims to bring together information across central and local government, has gone a long way to overcoming this need, but it still helps to understand what services are provided by which part of local government. Local authorities should also provide links on their websites to the appropriate authority for public services that are not their responsibility in order to direct people to the information they require. In some areas local portals have been developed which attempt to bring information together across the different tiers of local government and other parts of the public sector such as the police, e.g. *www.dorsetforyou.com* which covers all the local authorities in Dorset, or *www. lincup.net* which is described as 'Lincolnshire's electronic gateway', and *www.kentconnects.com* for Kent.

It is not possible to cover every category of local authority publishing in detail, and each authority publishes its own material so there is no central resource for a record of local authority output. There are, however, a number of categories of local authority publications which are worth discussing in some depth. These are:

- the formal record of the decision-making process
- research
- performance
- strategy and policy documents

- planning policy documents
- electoral registers.

There is legislation governing the formal record of an authority's decision-making process and a statutory requirement to produce certain plans and policies as well as the requirements of the Freedom of Information Act and the Environmental Information Regulations. Numerous other pieces of legislation or guidance require authorities to publish certain information but beyond that the authority can publish as much or as little as it chooses. In general local government, by its very nature, needs to issue substantial quantities of material mainly to ensure residents are aware of the services provided and how to access them. They will also need to promote changes in the way people behave such as encouraging recycling or promoting the use of sustainable travel options.

Publications and information

Formal record

The public record of an authority is held in the agendas and minutes of the council, its executive and its various committee meetings. Today the way in which these are published is set out by the Local Government (Access to Information) Act 1985 and availability has improved with the publication of council papers on the web. Keeping track of an authority's activities is easier with the web as you can view the agendas and minutes of meetings from your desk rather than having to visit a local authority office or library to view hard copies. However, the indexing and/or performance of the search engines on local authority websites still mean that accessibility could be improved.

The Local Government (Access to Information) Act 1985 requires authorities to make agendas, reports, background papers and minutes of the previous meeting available five clear days before a meeting. Papers can be designated as exempt (in effect confidential) but only if they meet the criteria set out in the Act. This is chiefly designed to protect individuals or the authority in, for instance, circumstances where the publication of the information would be prejudicial to the functioning of the authority.

Legislation also sets out how local authorities must make financial information available. The Audit Commission Act 1998 entitles members of the public to view local government financial accounts for a period of 20 days during the audit. Since December 2010, in an attempt to improve transparency, local authorities have been required to publish details of all expenditure over £500. This information has been made available on the websites of local authorities and provides the public with a list of suppliers and payments.

Research

Many local authorities undertake research in order to inform decisions made on developing, delivering and directing their services. This research may have a value beyond that for which it was conducted and its publication on websites and in print makes it available to a wider audience. Research is closely aligned with consultation work and the details of consultations being undertaken by local authorities and their outcomes are also included on their websites.

There has been a move to provide much of this research through what are known as local 'observatories'. Although these vary from one area to another in the way they are set up and managed, they often include a web-based data store and as such can provide a very useful resource. The type of information provided is largely statistical and will include the local analysis of the Census of Population, indices of multiple deprivation, educational attainment, health data and crime data, consultation results and other measures which can be used to judge the quality of life of residents of an area.

'Observatories' may well be made up of a local authority working with strategic partners from elsewhere in the public sector such as health and the police. Not all areas have set up observatories and the level of research capacity in local authorities varies. However, the development of strategic partnerships is increasingly leading to the creation of observatories to inform their work.

You can see examples at:

- *www.cambridgeshire.gov.uk/observatory*
- *www.northamptonshireobservatory.org.uk*
- *www.suffolkobservatory.info/*
- *www.warwickshireobservatory.org*

For more information on local authority research visit *www. laria.gov.uk* or *www.lgar.local.gov.uk*.

Some of the research undertaken by local authorities is a statutory requirement and LARIA (the Local Authority Research and Intelligence Association) in conjunction with the Local Government Association (LGA) published a guide to the statutory requirements for research in 2003 (*Statutory Requirements for Research. A Review of Responsibilities for English and Welsh Authorities*). This review covers only England and Wales but a Scottish equivalent is planned.

The review was limited to primary legislation since 1980 but still found extensive requirements for research, both explicit and implicit, in legislation relating to the functions of local authorities. It identified a requirement for research in preparing policy plans, statutory powers to undertake research in other areas and implicit requirements in many other functions.

In preparing policy plans the review found that it was a statutory requirement to undertake research in the areas of:

- housing needs
- air quality management
- waste recycling plans
- unitary development plans
- structure plans and local plans
- crime and disorder plans.

Many of the other policy documents an authority is required to produce do not have a clear legislative requirement for research but the need to undertake research is implicit in the task. This is true for instance in:

- homelessness strategies as required by the Homelessness Act 2002;
- local transport plans as required by the Transport Act 2000; and
- the accessibility strategies required as part of the Special Educational Needs and Disability Act 2001.

Local government statistics

Statistics are covered more thoroughly in the next chapter but it is worth making reference here to local authority statistics. Statistics about many aspects of the work of local authorities are published, but in many cases these will be aggregated to provide national figures based on returns made by the local authority to central government. This is true, for example, in areas such as casualty reduction figures, educational attainment, land use, housing and homelessness – in fact, for all the services provided by local government but where central government needs to be able to show how the nation is performing.

In recognition of the close relationship between central and local government statistics, CLIP, the Central and Local Information Partnership, was set up at the end of the 1990s. It aims to help central and local government work more closely together to collect, publish and use statistics (*www. clip.local.gov.uk*).

Local authorities issue their own figures as they are keen to show how they are performing. These are published both on their website and also in reports to council and other publications. Everyone is interested in what they receive for their council tax and authorities will also publish information about their performance. It is a statutory duty for local authorities to issue a leaflet giving outline information about their income and expenditure, and this will accompany the council tax bills when they are distributed at the beginning of each new financial year.

Performance and inspection information

Measuring the way an authority is performing may be undertaken by the research team within a local authority or by staff involved in other areas such as consultation. This may be for the authority's own performance management or may be required by the Audit Commission which has had responsibility for overseeing the work of local authorities in England and Wales. The Audit Commission can require an authority to publish information which will facilitate the comparison of an authority's performance with other authorities or with other years. From 2012 the Audit

Commission will no longer exist and the Coalition government has made extensive changes to the performance reporting required of local authorities in an attempt to make authorities more locally accountable.

The Audit Commission had also been charged with the inspection of local authorities as a whole so it is a useful source of information about authorities and specifically their performance. The Comprehensive Performance Assessment (CPA) introduced in 2002 was replaced in 2009 by the Comprehensive Area Assessment (CAA) which, as the name implies, looks at performance across the public sector in a specific geographic area. With the abolition of the Audit Commission, comparisons may be more difficult to make.

The Audit Commission website at *www.audit-commission. gov.uk* currently gives access to reports on local authorities via a search by authority name or by postcode, or by way of an alphabetical list. Searching by postcode will give you both authorities if you live in an area with two-tier local government. The site includes historical data back to 2002, links to reports for other tiers of local government in the area and other inspections carried out on the authority such as highways or libraries. The new inspection regime, introduced in 2009, moved away from measuring the performance of local authorities by using about 1,200 best value performance indicators. Instead, a set of 198 measures known as National Indicators were developed and then reduced in the budget of 2010 by 18. The Comprehensive Area Assessment (CAA) examined the quality of life for local people, whether the services they need are provided by the local authority or by other bodies. It recognised that, increasingly, local services are provided by partnerships, and Local Area Agreements (LAAs) were put in place in all areas of England to identify priorities for an area as agreed by central government, the local authority and other organisations involved in the delivery of public services. LAAs have now been discontinued. In Scotland the equivalent to LAAs are Single Outcome Agreements (SOAs) and they have been developed as the result of a concordat signed between the Scottish Government and local authorities in 2007. The SOAs are published on the website of the Improvement Service at *www.improvementservice.org.uk/single-outcome-agreements*.

This whole area is changing rapidly and it is important to check the current situation on the website of the Department for Communities and Local Government (*www.communities.gov.uk*). Government policy is to give local people a greater influence in the way local services are provided. These developments are as a result principally of the Lyons Inquiry into Local Government. The inquiry had its own website which has been archived by the UK Web Archiving Consortium – an example of web content which might otherwise have been lost (see *www.lyonsenquiry.org.uk*). The final report was issued in March 2007 and called *Place-shaping: A Shared Ambition for the Future of Local Government*. The latest step along the way at the time of writing has been the publication of a White Paper entitled *Communities in Control: Real People, Real Power*. In the context of this book, this White Paper is significant as it contains a chapter on access to information and states that 'access to information is a pre-requisite of community empowerment'. It sets out the need for local information in particular and ways of overcoming the barriers to accessing information such as social exclusion. It promises that the government will, for instance, encourage innovative use of new technologies and media and provide digital mentors to help groups in deprived areas set up websites.

Alongside the reporting on targets required by the Audit Commission, local authorities have long had to report on their performance to central government departments. From 2010 this, too, has been reduced with a 'single national dataset' agreed between central and local government, and local authorities will be compensated if departments ask for data over and above this.

Strategies and policy documents

In the recent past, the list of strategy and policy documents that local authorities were required to produce became very long. Although this has now been reduced, there are still many which are a statutory requirement and others that are considered good practice. A statutory requirement exists for documents such as:

- local air quality action plans
- waste recycling plans
- children's services plans
- health improvement and modernisation plans
- youth justice plans
- civil defence plans
- annual library plans
- accessibility strategies (access to schools for children with disabilities)
- class sizes plans
- behaviour support plans
- early years development and childcare plans
- Ofsted action plans and school organisations plans.

Other plans are usually produced as the result of guidance issued by central government, possibly in circulars or in order to secure funding.

Continuous change makes it very difficult to produce an authoritative list of what is currently required. For instance, under the Crime and Disorder Act 1998 each district, borough and unitary authority was required to work with the county councils and the police to develop a three-year crime and disorder strategy. It was designed to set out how they intended to address priorities identified from a crime audit and monitor performance against the strategy. The responsible authorities formed Crime and Disorder Partnerships to carry out the audits and produce the strategies. From 2007, the Police and Justice Act 2006 remove the duty for three-yearly crime and disorder strategies so those for 2005–08 were the last to be produced. However, the new legislation extends the scope of the Crime and Disorder Reduction Partnerships and requires them to produce an annual strategic assessment and annual three-year rolling plans. The legislation (The Crime and Disorder (Formulation and Implementation of Strategy) Regulations 2007 SI 2007/1830) describes these as partnership plans. This is a common problem with documents such as these where the thinking and subsequently the legislation or guidance change, and a series of documents which have been in existence for a few years are replaced by something similar but different.

Similarly, local air quality action plans were required for all areas that had identified an air quality management area (AQMA). An AQMA is an area where it is anticipated that national air quality objectives will not be met. However, as with local transport plans and a number of other plans, under the Local Authorities' Plans and Strategies (Disapplication) (England) Order 2005 authorities rated as 'excellent' under section 99(4) of the Local Government Act 2003 were no longer required to produce these plans. What complicates matters is that the Comprehensive Performance Assessment of local authorities is a rolling programme and an authority judged to be excellent at one inspection may not retain that level of achievement at the next inspection. The 2005 order applies to

- homelessness strategies
- home energy conservation reports
- youth justice plans
- rights of way improvement plans
- local transport plans and bus strategies and as described above
- air quality plans.

It would be inappropriate and impossible to try to cover all the plans produced by local authorities, but knowing of their existence could help in identifying an authority's approach to a particular issue. Just one of the more substantial plans has been examined in more detail here.

Examples

Local transport plans

Local transport plans (LTPs) are a requirement of the Transport Act 2000 and the legislation applies to county councils, unitary authorities and Passenger Transport Executives in metropolitan areas who work with the district councils. The legislation does not apply to London and, as indicated above, does not apply to those authorities which achieved an 'excellent' rating in the Comprehensive Performance Assessment of 2004. Interestingly, all the authorities exempt from producing an LTP have opted to continue to develop one.

The intention of an LTP is to set out how an authority plans to tackle local transport over the next five years and how it will implement its strategy. LTPs are submitted to the

Department for Transport (DfT) who will use the information to allocate capital funding and develop their own policies on local transport issues. Progress in implementing the plan is monitored by the DfT and annual progress reports are published by the local authorities and Passenger Transport Executives.

Local transport plans are available on local authority websites but are often very large documents so can be slow to download if provided simply as a PDF. Some authorities provide html versions and the plan may be available on a CD. The plans produced by Passenger Transport Executives have their own websites such as those for Greater Manchester at *www.gmltp.co.uk*, West Yorkshire at *www.wyltp.com* and the West of England at *www.westofengland.org*.

Planning policy

The Planning and Compulsory Purchase Act 2004 changed the way in which local authorities develop and communicate their planning policies.

Alongside these changes, work on delivering e-planning as part of e-government was designed to make information about planning applications and the process of applying for planning permission available electronically.

For planning policy, until 2004, a Structure Plan produced by the county or unitary authority for an area was the overarching document supported by local plans at district level where appropriate. The Structure Plan was developed within the context of the Regional Planning Guidance issued by the government office for the region and the Planning Policy Guidance issued by central government. It set out how it was intended that an area should develop.

The Planning and Compulsory Purchase Act 2004 replaced structure plans and local plans with a set of documents known as the Local Development Framework and a document called the Regional Spatial Strategy.

The Local Development Framework is a folder of documents produced by district councils, unitary authorities and the national parks. They set out the spatial planning strategy for the area. The Regional Spatial Strategy includes details of transport, waste, energy and minerals but the Coalition government quickly announced plans to scrap these when it was elected and their demise is included in the Localism Bill.

The Local Development Framework consists of three required documents:

- Statement of Community Involvement (which sets out an authority's standards for involving the community in plan preparation and review)
- Annual Monitoring Report
- Local Development Scheme

and optional documents:

- Supplementary planning documents, e.g. Oxford City Council Affordable House Supplementary Planning Document
- Local Development Orders
- Simplified Planning Zones.

The documents are described in more detail in *Planning Policy Statement 12: Local Development Frameworks*.

The Minerals and Waste Development Framework replaced the Waste Local Plan and the Minerals Local Plan.

An annotated guide to the Local Development Framework is available on the Planning Portal website at *www. planningportal.gov.uk*. Planning policy locally is developed within the recommendations of the Planning Policy Guidance, issued by the government on topics such as housing, flooding, green belts, transport and telecommunications. These are gradually being replaced by Planning Policy Statements and, unlike the Regional Planning Guidance, are being re-written and re-issued. A full list of the current documents can be found on the website of DCLG at *www.communities.gov.uk*.

The Planning Act 2008 provided for the creation of an independent Infrastructure Planning Commission which is responsible for making decisions on major infrastructure projects of national importance. The decisions are made in line with the National Planning Policy Statements and local authorities are consulted but the final decision rests with the Commission. This Act also made it a requirement that Regional Spatial Strategies and Development Plan Documents contribute to policy on climate change and introduced the Community Infrastructure Levy which allows local authorities to charge developers for the provision of the necessary infrastructure to support a development.

Scotland

In Scotland, strategic planning underwent a major overhaul under the Planning etc. (Scotland) Act 2006. The system is based on structure plans and 17 areas were identified in the Town and Country Planning (Scotland) Act 1997 as needing to produce them. The Act specified that they cover 'general development and land use policies'. These are being replaced with Strategic Development Plans (SDPs) which for the four major city regions of Scotland are to be known as City Region Plans (CRPs) and in all other areas as Local Development Plans (LDPs).

A National Planning Framework was published in 2004 with a programme of reviews every four years. It sets out plans for spatial development in Scotland until 2025. It was developed and managed by the Scottish Government and the 2006 planning act gave it statutory status.

Wales

In Wales, strategic planning is covered by the Planning and Compulsory Purchase Act 2004 and the same pattern of development documents applies as in England.

Northern Ireland

In Northern Ireland, strategic planning is the responsibility of the Northern Ireland Department for the Environment. Legislation and planning policy is the responsibility of the Northern Ireland Assembly, with the Department for the Environment creating a Regional Development Strategy and Development Plans.

Electoral registers

Local authorities have responsibility for organising all types of elections. This includes the election of councillors, elected mayors, Members of Parliament (MPs) and Members of the European Parliament (MEPs), and managing referenda. In Wales, Scotland and Northern Ireland they will also manage the election of members of the devolved assemblies.

An essential part of the process is the maintenance of electoral registers for the area and this function rests with district or unitary authorities. Having a list of every member of the population who is eligible to vote is essential for the conduct of elections but is also a very useful source of information for use in other areas of life such as credit checks, marketing and tracing individuals. However, the information is not made available as widely as some would like and there are restrictions on its use.

The way in which electoral registers are now managed was mainly laid down in the Representation of the People Act 2000. The major change brought about by this act was the move from a register created on one date each year to a rolling register to which electors can be added at any point during the year. There was also the requirement for local authorities to produce two editions of the register. One copy is the full list of all electors to be used at elections, made available for public inspection and supplied to certain bodies either free of charge or for a fee. The other version is edited to exclude the names of those who have opted, when completing the electoral registration form, to have their names withheld. Local authorities can supply the edited version to anyone requesting it and charge a fee.

The full copy is supplied to credit checking companies and public libraries. Regulations prevent the copying of the full register. This has caused problems for public libraries where full copies of the register are held and where staff must ensure no copying takes place. It has also resulted in some authorities not supplying copies of the full register to libraries, and concerns about access to the register for electors to check they are included and their details are correct. If the register is not available in a public library a visit to the local authority offices may be required and this may need to be made during office hours, which may be shorter than those of the public library.

The Data Sharing Review published in July 2008 recommended that local authorities should no longer be allowed to sell the edited version of the register. As the sole purpose of the edited register is to provide a version which can be sold for use by anyone, this change would mean that there would be no point in producing the edited version.

The argument supporting this is that under the Data Protection Act information should be collected and processed for a particular and limited purpose. In selling copies of the edited register it is argued that personal information collected for a particular purpose, i.e. the democratic process, is then being sold on to anyone who can use it for any purpose. The Ministry of Justice is consulting on a way forward, with six options, half of which involve abolishing the edited register. (See *www.justice.gov.uk*.)

Further changes were made to the process as a result of the Electoral Administration Act 2006, including a move to create a central register held electronically. This would be a Coordinated Online Record of Electors or CORE. The act provided for one or more CORE schemes to be created and run by a keeper, which could be the Electoral Commission. In 2011 this scheme was discontinued.

Despite the best efforts of electoral registration officers, it is inevitable that some eligible voters will not register even though registration is compulsory. This act established a new duty on electoral registration officers to register eligible voters. Previously the responsibility rested with the elector who, if they failed to register, could be fined but perhaps more importantly would lose their democratic right to vote. (Failing to register can also affect your credit rating as credit checking agencies use electoral registers.) In using electoral registers the limitations of the data included should be understood.

Superseded registers are a valuable source of information for people tracing family history or doing other research, and a complete set is kept by the British Library. Under the Representation of the People legislation, the British Library received a complete set of electoral registers for the whole of the United Kingdom (England, Wales, Scotland and Northern Ireland) from and including 1947. From 2003 the Library holds the full, but not the edited, version of the register. The British Library's holdings are listed in *Parliamentary Constituencies and Their Registers Since 1832* which also lists non-Parliamentary registers (burgess rolls, jurors lists, valuation rolls, etc.) and poll books held by the Library. The registers are held by the Social Sciences and Official Publications Reading Room but can only be consulted (under supervision) by personal visitors to the Reading Rooms and can only be copied by hand. The law prevents the Library from disclosing any information from the full version over the telephone or in writing so a visit to the Reading Room is essential to access the information.

In the digital age this approach seems rather archaic which is why the edited version is available for purchase and is made available electronically by a number of agencies. 192. com (*www.192.com*), for instance, allows searching of the edited registers from the current register back to 2002 for a fee. More information about available sources of electoral registers is maintained on the British Library website at *www.bl.uk* and the BL is working with *findmypast.co.uk* to digitise the electoral registers from 1832–1932.

Local authority archives

Local authority archives or record offices hold the official record of the decisions made by an authority but also a wealth of information about the lives of ordinary people and businesses in the area. There are more than 130 local authorities providing archive services and the collections include photos, maps, plans, and audio recordings and are a valuable resource. For more information go to *www.archiveawareness.com*.

The Fire Service

There are currently 63 fire brigades in the UK although this is under review. During the war years from 1938 to 1947 there was a National Fire Service (NFS) and an Auxiliary Fire Service (AFS) but under the Fire Services Act 1947, county council and county borough brigades were established.

A directory with contact details for each fire service is available at *www.fireservice.co.uk/information/ukfrs.php*, a site developed and provided by fire officers for the public and their colleagues.

Each fire service either has its own website or offers information as part of the appropriate County Council website, e.g. *www.leicestershire-fire.gov.uk/*.

A useful source of information about the fire service is the website of the Fire Service College which is located in Moreton-in-Marsh, Gloucestershire, and its library which has an online catalogue is considered to be the best specialist library on fire topics (*www.fireservicecollege.ac.uk*). Fire services are required to produce an integrated risk management plan which sets out how they intend to manage fire risk and other emergencies. They also publish policies and advice and guidance. A useful guide to the Fire Service in the UK is included on the Directgov website alongside advice on fire safety.

Finding local authority information

Search engines and navigation on local authority websites

There is no standard search engine used on local authority websites and the quality of results varies. The navigation of local authority websites also varies in its usability. Attempts have been made to standardise the navigation and the subject metadata of local authority websites, and use of the Integrated Public Sector Vocabulary (IPSV) in the subject field of the metadata was a requirement by the end of 2006.

Local authority publications are subject to Legal Deposit and may therefore be included in the British National Bibliography (BNB) but for practical reasons the British Library limits the material it collects. It is also clear that many local authorities are unaware of their legal deposit responsibilities.

There is no single listing of local authority publications. The British Library's SIGLE (System for Information on Grey Literature) included selective local authority publications until 2003 but then stopped, and the service itself was discontinued in 2006.

In an attempt to make local government information easier to find, the *Guidelines for Official Publications in Local Authorities* was issued in 2007. The Guidelines were published by the LGA working with the National Foundation for Educational Research (NFER), the Affiliation of Local Government Information Specialists (ALGIS) and the Standing Committee on Official Publications (SCOOP). The publication and related website attempt to steer those responsible for local authority publications into good practice in publishing information. The Guidelines are available as a pdf and a web tool which will be updated by NFER at *www.nfer.ac.uk/LAPublishing*.

Other technologies

Local authorities, keen to reach those without web access, are making use of other technologies. This includes *Looking Local*, the local government digital TV portal which provides access to some local authority information through digital TV services such as Sky. Similarly, kiosks are used to provide limited information for people out and about.

Text messaging or SMS (Short Message Service) is used to allow members of the public to report faults such as potholes or faulty streetlights, for tenants to request services or provide information but also for local authorities to convey information to their citizens. It is used, for instance, to inform parents and children of school closures and to contact parents of absent children who haven't told the school that their child will not be in school that day. It is making use of the technology most likely to be available to both the adult population and to children. Figures from the Office for National Statistics show ownership of mobile phones at 81 per cent by 2009 for UK households, and 93 per cent of homes with two adults and two children had Internet access. Of course, these technologies are now merging with the introduction of smart phones.

Linked to this is the increasing use of call centres which are designed to improve customer access to information while freeing up professional staff.

Although not perhaps in the same category, local authorities are making use of GIS or Geographical Information Systems on their websites to display information about their area on mapping tools. This may be road works information, details of planning applications or local authority facilities such as libraries, recycling centres or parks. It may also be used to allow residents to search for their local councillor by postcode or to find their nearest facilities.

Further information

For a pocket history of the development of local government see the Local Government Association (LGA) *Key dates in English and Welsh Local Government History* available on their website at *www.lga.gov.uk*.

For the structure of local government see *Local Government Structure* also produced by the LGA and on their website, and *Types and Names of Local Authorities in England and Wales* which gives the detail.

Local Authority Services by the LGA gives an overview of services provided by local government.

Directory information about local authorities

Municipal Year Book

For directory information about local authorities, the *Municipal Year Book* is a long established source. The hard-copy version is published each year but there is also a web-based subscription service available at *www.LocalGov.co.uk*. This service includes news, jobs, events and discussion forums and a wiki of local government-related terms.

Directory of Local Authorities

Published annually in hardback and on CD-ROM by Sweet & Maxwell, the *Directory* is particularly aimed at the legal profession and especially those doing conveyancing work or requiring local authority searches. It covers England, Scotland and Wales.

Local Government Chronicle

The publishers of the *Local Government Chronicle*, a weekly magazine aimed at local authority staff, have for many years operated a news service which covers news and events related to local government. They too publish a directory of local authorities at *www.lgcnet.com* and news and information on subscription at *www.lgcplus.com*.

The London Councils

Formerly the Association of London Government, the London Councils have directory information on their website at *www.londoncouncils.gov.uk*.

The Convention of Scottish Local Authorities (COSLA)

COSLA represents the Scottish unitary authorities. It publishes a *Directory of Scottish Local Government* which is made available as a hard-copy publication and on CD (*www.cosla.gov.uk*).

Nibusinessinfo.co.uk provides contact information for local authorities in Northern Ireland.

Information *for* local government

There are a number of organisations which provide information services *for* local authorities, usually as part of a wider role.

Local Government Association (LGA)

(*www.lga.gov.uk*)

The largest and best known is the LGA which represents all local authorities in England and Wales. Formed in 1997, it exists to 'promote better local government'. It has a publishing programme ranging from research to leaflets on current topics and a number of information services. The LGA website is a useful source of information about local government itself as well as providing information to local government. The website has both public and member-only content, and publications are available to order or download.

The LGA through LGConnect provides an information service, which includes a weekly magazine for councillors and a variety of electronic alerting services. A daily headlines service covers local government-related news in the press and *LGalerts* summarise topical issues such as the publication of a White Paper, new legislation, conferences and consultation. A weekly checklist of these is also circulated by email. Monthly bulletins are produced by the LGA Boards, which have particular areas of interest, e.g. community well-being, regeneration or domestic violence.

The LGA works with a number of other organisations which are known as the LGA Group. These are:

- Improvement and Development Agency for local government (IDeA) (*www.idea.gov.uk*).
- Local Government Employers (LGE) (*www.lge.gov.uk*).
- Public Private Partnerships Programme (4ps) (*www.4ps. gov.uk*).
- Local Authority Coordinators of Regulatory Services (LACORS) (*www.lacors.gov.uk*).
- The Leadership Centre for Local Government (*www. localleadership.gov.uk*).

Local Government Analysis and Research (*www.lgar.local. gov.uk*) is the research arm of the LGA and works with other organisations to 'improve and develop evidence, data and research to support the local government sector; and ensure that the sector can access and benefit from this resource'.

Local Government Information Unit (LGIU)

(*www.lgiu.gov.uk*)

This body undertakes research and provides information services for local government. It is best known for its policy briefings on relevant legislation and proposed changes to government policy.

National Association of Local Councils

(*www.nalc.gov.uk*)

The equivalent body to the LGA at the parish, town and community level is the NALC and each area will have a local association, e.g. Warwickshire and West Midlands Association of Local Councils (WALC) at *www.walc.org.uk*. NALC publishes guidance for parish clerks and the *Local Council Review,* all of which is now available electronically.

Info4local

(*www.Info4local.gov.uk*)

This service provides information for local government from central government and is particularly useful for keeping abreast of publications through email alerts and especially consultations, as it lists new consultations and those about to close.

Wired-gov

(*www.wired-gov.net*)

Wired-gov provides an email alerting service in conjunction with the Central Office of Information and many other organisations in central government, and increasingly the wider public sector. Free to the public sector and on subscription to the private sector, it includes a weekly newsletter, *WG Plus*, which provides a round-up of the week's news.

Case studies

To illustrate some of the uses which may be made of local authority information, a number case studies have been included here.

Who is my councillor?

A resident with serious concerns about parking in their road due to parents depositing and collecting children from a nearby school wants to find out what can be done to improve the situation. He lives in an area with a county council and a district council so he visits the *www.direct.gov.uk* website and searches by his postcode to find the right authority. This gives him links to both authorities but he still doesn't know which one he needs. He selects the district council and is offered a link to their home page or a contact page. He goes to the home page and searches for 'parking' but finds only information on resident parking permits, on-street parking charges and penalties, and Blue Badges. The FAQs don't help either. He then looks at the website for his local county council and again searches by 'parking'. He fares no better and decides he will need to speak to his local councillor. He returns to the district council site and under 'Council and Democracy' or similar heading finds a postcode search which gives him his district councillor and his telephone number. He phones but is told he needs to speak to his county councillor and is given the details so at least he doesn't need to go back to the website again! His county councillor is able to tell him that the issue has already been raised and a report will be considered by the council's cabinet in a couple of months on some actions to be taken to improve the situation. He is told that the report will appear on the website of the county council at least five days before the meeting so he can read it for himself.

How do I apply for planning consent to extend my home?

A resident wants to add a conservatory to his property but he has been told it will require planning consent. Again he lives in an area with a two-tier local government structure so will first need to know which authority to approach. The resident finds this information quite easily by using Google to search for 'planning permission UK' which takes him to the Planning Portal at *www.planningportal.gov.uk*. Selecting the section of the site for the general public, he finds he can search by postcode and quickly finds a clear explanation of which authority he needs to go to for permission. The site explains that it will be the district or borough council which deals with small-scale residential applications. The county council handles minerals and waste planning and planning applications for schools etc. (This is, of course, easier in areas with unitary authorities where all services are provided by one authority.)

He also finds that they accept applications online and he is able to do this from the Planning Portal site after he has registered, which isn't difficult. He also finds an interactive 'house' which tells him more about planning permission and the building regulations for conservatories and many other additions and alterations to houses. Having submitted his application, he also finds he can pay online.

Initially he wanted to check to see what development is being permitted in the area and the Planning Portal tells him he can identify this through the local plan and the other documents, which make up the Local Development Framework. The Planning Portal includes links to development plans but unfortunately there were none available for his local authority. However, he finds them by visiting the local authority's own site later.

Having submitted his application, he will want to keep track of its progress. If the decision cannot be made by the planning officers under delegated powers, it will need to be considered by the planning committee. The local authority website gives the details of the committee dates and times and information about being allowed to speak for three minutes, and the Planning Portal allows him to log in and see what progress his application has made.

What does my local authority do about recycling?

As a very topical issue, you should find a wealth of information on this subject on the websites of unitary, district, borough *and* county authorities. This is because waste collection and waste management are the responsibilities of different tiers of local government. Unitary authorities, of course, cover both aspects of waste but in two-tier areas the district or borough will collect the waste while the county will manage its disposal. It is in the interests of all authorities, therefore, to encourage the reduction of waste through recycling, not least because of the costs of collecting and disposing of it, but also because of the steady increase in landfill tax which waste management authorities have to pay for each tonne of waste which ends up in a landfill site.

References

Note: Legislation is available on the Official Legislation at at *www.legislation.gov.uk* and is not listed here.

Department of Communities and Local Government (2006) *Strong and Prosperous Communities – The Local Government White Paper.* London: TSO.

Department of Communities and Local Government (2008) *Communities in Control: Real People, Real Power.* London: TSO.

Department of Transport, Local Government and the Regions (1998) *Modern Local Government: In Touch with the People.*

HM Government and the LGA (2007) *Central–Local Concordat,* 12 December. Online at: *www.communities. gov.uk.*

HM Treasury, Department for Business, Enterprise and Regulatory Reform and Department for Communities and Local Government (2007) *Review of Sub-national Economic Development and Regeneration July 2007.* London: TSO. Online at: *www.hm-treasury.gov.uk.*

House of Commons Library (2008) *The Central–Local Concordat,* Nicola Headlam (Standard Note SN/PC/04713).

Local Authority Research and Intelligence Association and Local Government Association (2003) *Statutory Requirements for Research: A Review of Responsibilities for English and Welsh Local Government.* London: LGA.

Local Government Association *Key dates in English and Welsh Local Government History.* Online at: *www.lga.gov.uk.*

Local Government Association *Local Authority Services.* Online at: *www.lga.gov.uk.*

Local Government Association. *Types and Names of Local Authorities in England and Wales.* Online at: *www.lga.gov.uk.*

Lyons, Sir Michael (2007) *Place-shaping: A Shared Ambition for the Future of Local Government* (the Lyons Report).

Planning Policy Statement 12: *Local Development Frameworks.*

Thomas, Richard and Walport, Mark (2008) *Data Sharing Review Report.* Online.

8

Statistics

This chapter covers:

- introduction;
- history of official statistics;
- overview of official statistics;
- national statistics on the web;
- other sources of official statistics;
- census and neighbourhood statistics;
- using official statistics;
- issues affecting official statistics;
- case study on housing statistics.

Introduction

British official statistics cover every aspect of life, and statistics produced by the British government and other official bodies in this country are of fundamental importance for monitoring economic and social developments and the changes taking place in society. It would be impossible in a short chapter to offer detailed guidance on the vast array of statistics available so the aim here, as with the rest of the book, is to:

- provide pointers to what is published both by the Office for National Statistics and other public sector organisations;
- offer help in making use of these resources;
- warn of the pitfalls to avoid.

The Government Statistical Service (GSS) explains that 'official statistics are provided to inform debate, decision-making and research both within government and by the wider community'. The government is sometimes the only entity with the authority to collect some statistics and the population census is an example of this. There is also a legal responsibility on government to collect statistics. The Census of Production Act 1906 laid down that the Board of Trade should conduct a census of industrial production in the UK, the Statistics of Trade Act 1947 provided for the Board of Trade to carry out a census of distribution to add to statistics on national output and incidentally required businesses to respond to survey requests from the Board. It is the Census Act 1920 which makes provision for government to undertake a census from time to time although it does not require a census.

Every book on statistics is likely to quote Disraeli's remark on lies, damn lies and statistics. Like many aphorisms, there is some truth in it. It is certainly true to say that statistics are only as good as the sources upon which they are based and it may not be easy or possible in some cases to count accurately what needs to be counted. Those who produce official statistics pride themselves on their professionalism and independence. That is not to say that one should not show some scepticism when dealing with statistics. Some misplaced criticism can come from the media which either misunderstands the nature of the statistical process or, it has to be said, selects only the figures which suit its agenda.

The UK National Statistics website is the single most important source of official statistics for the UK but it is only part of the picture. Many government departments and a range of official bodies such as the Bank of England and the Civil Aviation Authority collect and publish specialist statistics. The devolved administrations in Scotland, Wales and Northern Ireland offer detailed data on their own countries and Eurostat, the Statistical Office of the European Union, harmonises and publishes much statistical data about Britain where it can be seen in comparison with other member states.

History of official statistics

Attempts at collecting official statistics in Great Britain may be traced back to the eighteenth century. The first decennial census, for instance, was undertaken in 1801 although the first recognisably 'modern' census was that conducted in 1841. Economic statistics were first collected in the 1830s by the Board of Trade when it established its statistical department and 1854 saw the first publication of the *Statistical Abstract of the United Kingdom* which is still published today as the *Annual Abstract*.

However, there were shortcomings with the organisation and collection of government statistics and a call was made in 1880 for a central statistical office to be created. This was rejected but finally in 1941, faced with inter-departmental confusion during the early stages of the Second World War, Winston Churchill set up the Central Statistical Office (CSO). After the war the CSO began to expand, principally to produce national accounts statistics which would contribute to the management of the economy.

In the late 1960s, there was an increase in the range of statistics and distinct improvements in their quality. In 1986, the remit of the Director of the CSO was broadened and the job holder became the Head of the Government Statistical Service. This encompassed the statisticians serving across Whitehall and not just those working for the CSO. The Business Statistics Office (BSO) was created in 1969 and the Office of Population Censuses and Surveys (OPCS) in 1970, while in the 1980s Mrs Thatcher instituted a review of statistics. The *Rayner Review* was undertaken by Sir Derek Rayner and designed to save money. It was essentially an attempt to reduce costs by restricting the collection of statistics to those required by the government itself. By the mid-1980s there had been a marked deterioration in the quality of the national accounts data and, as a result of a Treasury and Civil Service Committee recommendation, the government announced a Cabinet Office review which reported that the causes of the deterioration were many and of long standing (*Government Economic Statistics: A Scrutiny Report*). The majority of the recommendations made by the report were implemented and the CSO was moved from the control of the Cabinet Office to the aegis of the Treasury. In 1996 the Office for National Statistics, an Executive Agency accountable to the Chancellor of the Exchequer, was established. It was created through the merger of the CSO and the OPCS, with the Director of the ONS acting as the Registrar General for England and Wales as well as the Head of the GSS. In the *Framework for National Statistics* published in 2000 the government added the title of National Statistician to that of the Director. This document also created the concept of 'national statistics' – a designated set of statistics – and established a new body, the Statistics Commission, to act as an independent check on the integrity of official statistics.

The latest stage in the long history of official statistics was the passing of the Statistics and Registration Service Act of 2007 which created the UK Statistics Authority, a non-ministerial department accountable to Parliament. The Authority, according to its website, 'is the legal successor to ONS, which has in turn become an "executive office"'. The Authority also absorbed the role performed by the Statistics Commission and its responsibilities cover the entire UK statistical system (*www.statistics.gov.uk*). Its remit extends to Scotland, Wales and Northern Ireland.

Overview of official statistics

Statistics are published by many of the public sector bodies covered in this book so it is worth considering here the statistics issued by:

- Parliament at Westminster;
- devolved Parliament and Assemblies;
- UK central government departments;
- other public bodies including the National Health Service and Police;
- regional bodies including the Greater London Authority;
- local government including the Fire Service.

It is important to know what is issued by each of these bodies and how to find the material. With the introduction of the UK Statistics Authority website much of the previously dispersed statistical information has been brought together but there is still much that is not available through this route.

Parliament

You will often find some very useful statistics brought together as the response to a Parliamentary question and therefore published in *Hansard*. These may be on almost any topic and may be information which has been brought together specifically to respond to the question and is not available anywhere else. However, they may not be very easy to find as they will be linked to Parliamentary questions and not published as statistics as such.

There are many statistics about Parliament itself and how it functions and these are mainly brought together in the *Sessional Information Digest* referred to in Chapter 3 on Parliament at Westminster.

Devolved Parliament and Assemblies

The devolved administrations in Scotland, Wales and Northern Ireland are responsible for the collection and publication of statistics for their own areas and contribute data to the UK Statistics Authority. However, they publish most statistics about their areas themselves.

For Scotland there is a Statisticians Group which 'aims to provide relevant and reliable statistical information, analysis and advice to government, business and the people of Scotland'. At *www.scotland.gov.uk/topics/statistics* there is a range of statistics published by topic, e.g. Agriculture, Fisheries and Rural, Crime and Justice, Economy.

For Wales go to *www.wales.gov.uk/statistics* for information on how they collect and publish statistics and use StatsWales for data that can be viewed and manipulated and makes provision for advanced users.

In Northern Ireland statistics are managed by the Northern Ireland Statistics and Research Agency (NISRA) and their website *www.nisra.gov.uk* gives access to a full set of statistics to 'inform the policy process within Government, research within Academia and contribute to debate in the wider community'.

UK central government departments

Central government departments collect and publish data in their areas of responsibility and some of this is published as separate publications as well as being submitted to the UK Statistics Authority. Examples of detailed statistics published by government departments are those published by the Department for Transport at *www.dft.gov.uk/pgr/statistics* which include statistics for buses, congestion, road casualties, blue badges and much more and the Ministry of Justice at *www.justice.gov.uk/publications/statistics.htm* where statistics are published which cover many aspects of the criminal and civil justice system including knife possession, population in custody, reoffending, safety in custody and youth justice.

Social Trends is a well established publication of data on a range of social and economic topics covered by central government departments. It is published as a report and as the data on *www.statistics.gov.uk* and covers 'population, households and families, education and training, labour market, income and wealth, expenditure, health, social protection, crime and justice, housing, environment, transport, lifestyles and social participation'. Its advantage is that it brings together information from a range of government sources and covers a wide time span so it can be used to help understand how the country has developed and changed over 40 years in many aspects of life. Having comparative data when dealing with any statistics is essential as without being able to see how things have changed over time the value of any statistics is greatly reduced.

Other public bodies including the National Health Service and Police

Similarly to the central government departments, other public bodies will be required to submit statistics to the UK Statistics Authority but will also publish some themselves.

Examples here include the Metropolitan Police Force which at *www.met.police.uk/crimefigures* makes available crime figures for the area covered by the Force, and the NHS which at *www.ic.nhs.uk/statistics-and-data-collections* publishes a range of statistics on topics such as alcohol consumption, GPs' earnings, screening, social care and vacancies, turnover, sickness and absence for the workforce.

Although the UK Statistics Authority collects and publishes information from many of these areas, it is sometimes easier to find it on the websites of the government departments or public sector body as there are fewer topics covered and therefore less material to search through.

Regions in England including the Greater London Authority

Now that the regional assemblies have been abolished and the regional development agencies closed, the Office for National Statistics is the only source of regional statistics.

Regional Trends produced by the Office for National Statistics, published by Palgrave Macmillan and now into its 43rd edition, brings all this data and analysis together in one publication.

The Greater London Authority publishes statistical information about the area it covers and now this is often made available on the London data store site at *London.gov. uk/datastore*. The data sets are arranged alphabetically by title, by categories, by keywords and by organisations. There is a search facility and an opportunity to request data sets not yet available. This is the model now being emulated across the public sector.

Local government including the Fire Service and Police

Local authorities are required to make returns to central government departments for much of what they do. Their returns will be combined with information from other authorities to give a national picture but the detail will also be made available at the local level. They report on performance in areas such as road casualties, recycling, the state of the roads, the number of people helped back into work and much more – many to be set against national indicators. These will then be published as aggregated data in publications such as *Reported Road Casualties Great Britain* which is published by the Department for Transport and *Crime in England and Wales* published each year since 2000.

Crime in England and Wales is now available alongside the *National Crime Map* which is an online mapping tool that allows users to view crime data by postcode, town or police force. The information for both the publication and the map comes from combining the records of crime collected by the police and the information collected through the *British Crime Survey*. The website *www.police.uk* hosts the mapping tool which allows you to see crimes reported in a location by searching for a street name or postcode. When it was launched in February 2011 the site was receiving 75,000 hits per minute which is an example of how official data can be far from dull.

The moves to publish open data as in the London data store example mentioned above mean that local authorities are making available considerable amounts of data which was not previously published. It may not be particularly well indexed, and care is needed when using the data as described below in the section on using official statistics.

National statistics on the web

The increase in the quantity of government statistical information on the web and the fact that it is largely available free of charge for anyone to use has revolutionised access to official statistics over the past 15 years.

The UK National Statistics Publication Hub *www. statistics.gov.uk* is at the centre of this change, providing:

■ access to the latest statistical releases and a repository of statistical data from the Office for National Statistics; and

■ portal access to statistics on many other government websites.

It is described as the 'gateway to UK national statistics' and encompasses the Office for National Statistics now at *www. ons.gov.uk*.

Statistics are divided up by themes:

■ Agriculture and Environment   ■ Health and Social Care

■ Business and Energy   ■ Labour Market

■ Children, Education and Skills ■ People and Places

■ Crime and Justice   ■ Population

■ Economy   ■ Travel and Transport

■ Government

and cross-cutting topics such as equality and diversity and migration.

Recent releases are listed as news items on the home page and links take you to:

- a release calendar which allows you to see when to expect publication of particular statistics;
- details of the government statistics producers and other organisations which produce official statistics;
- a facility for browsing by theme which breaks down the top-level themes to a more detailed level;
- a link to regional statistics which allows you to look at data for a specific region of the UK.

The site is a hub and as such much of the information it links to is held on the websites of other government bodies. What is noticeable is that the information is not simply statistical tables. The links may well take you through to the Office for National Statistics where there are tables of data, but it may also link to a publication containing data sitting on the website of a government department. For example, following the links to 'People and Places' and then 'Households' will bring up material on affordable housing and one item here is the 'Affordable housing survey'. If you select 'Current and past editions' the link takes you to the website of the Homes and Communities Agency (HCA) and its list of publications. Scrolling down you will eventually find the document referred to and will be able to open or download it. There are clearly statistics in this report but it is far more than a statistical table.

Meanwhile, the site for the Office for National Statistics is also structured by themes which are similar but not identical to those of the hub. Under the title *UK Snapshot* are useful links to what are called 'Brief analysis'. These are popular topics where the data is presented in a chart and a brief interpretation is given. These can be particularly useful for anyone looking for basic information, perhaps to include in a report or support an assertion. Information may be found, for instance, on the number of overseas visitors to the UK over the past three years, the number of people with Internet access, Gross Domestic Product (GDP) growth or the index of production which shows production output for industry in the UK in manufacturing, mining and quarrying, and energy supply industries.

Another series of ONS publications in this section is called *Focus on* and they combine data from various sources to illustrate a topic such as older people, children, gender, health and many others and provide links to further information. *Brief Guides* are not the data but information about the data so that you know what it is, how it is collected and calculated and how to find it. Examples include the Retail Price Index (RPI), Profitability and Gross Domestic Product (GDP).

Finally in this section is the *Virtual Bookshelf* which provides access by theme to the actual data sets as well as reports, articles and news releases. It is important to read the introduction to the data sets so that you are clear about what is and isn't included, where the data has come from and how it is calculated. The *Virtual Bookshelf* is arranged by categories and each data set listed within the categories has a description of the type of content and the primary medium in which it is published, e.g. online, a summary description, price, the main area for which data is collected, frequency of release and the most recent year for which data is available. The categories covered are:

- Agriculture, Fishing and Forestry
- Commerce, Energy and Industry
- Compendia and Reference
- Crime and Justice
- Economy
- Education and Training
- Health and Care

- Labour Market
- Natural and Built Environment
- Population and Migration
- Public Sector and Other
- Social and Welfare
- Transport, Travel and Tourism.

The *Virtual Bookshelf* is a valuable resource providing access in a structured way to reliable retrospective data.

Census and Neighbourhood Statistics

The census is conducted every ten years in the UK and aims to cover 100 per cent of the population. It is carried out under the Census Act 1920 which covers England, Scotland and Wales and the Census Act (Northern Ireland) 1969. Its completion is compulsory. It surveys all people and households and provides essential information for the government of the country. It provides a wealth of information and is especially useful and well known for its use by family history researchers.

The exercise has been conducted since 1801 but greater detail has been collected since 1841, increasing again from 1951, the exception being the 1941 census when a reduced survey was conducted because of the war.

In 1920 the Census Act was passed which provided for the census to be closed for 100 years but in 2006 it was agreed by the Information Commissioner that as the 1911 census was not covered by the Act it should be made available early. It was published in 2009 but personally sensitive data was not available before the 100 years had passed. The information is available at *www.1911census.co.uk*. The National Archives has worked with partners to make census information available and the records back to 1841 are available from their website *www.nationalarchives.gov.uk*.

For Scottish censuses see *www.scotlandspeople.gov.uk* which gives access to these alongside the Statutory Registers, Parish Registers and Catholic Registers. In Scotland the 1911 census was not published until 2011.

In Northern Ireland the Public Record Office of Northern Ireland (*www.proni.gov.uk*) has responsibility for the preservation of records but as Ireland was not partitioned until 1922 the census records for 1901 and 1911 are available for both the north and the south on the site of the National Archives of Ireland at *www.nationalarchives.ie*. Sadly none of the census records for 1861, 1871, 1881 and 1891 have survived as once the data was taken from them they weren't considered to be worth keeping.

These sites give access to the detailed information collected as part of the census exercise, e.g. names, addresses, ages, occupations, etc. and they have a valuable historic use. However, the latest census provides the statistics needed by the government, businesses and the communities in which we live. It can be used to predict the population allowing the planning of, for instance, the provision of educational facilities and to track trends in employment, housing, ethnic make-up, etc.

For information about the census go to *www.ons.gov.uk/census* where you will find the data from the latest census set out as follow:

- Key Statistics (KS) – summary tables covering the most significant and requested counts.

- Standard Tables (ST) – the most detailed of all census tables. They are not produced for small areas.

- Census Area Statistics (CAS) – mostly versions of the Standard Tables for smaller areas, but containing less detail.

The site explains that the tables of data are produced for a number of area types, or geographies, such as local government, health administration, parliamentary constituencies, postcode sectors, urban areas, small neighbourhood areas, combined adjacent postcodes which form Output Areas (OAs) and OAs grouped into Super Output Areas. It is possible to select topics such as people, health, work, employment and crime and using a postcode or location name to see the figures for the area, set against the numbers or percentage for the local authority area and the region.

For instance, searching by postcode and selecting health, you may find that in your area 76.8 per cent of the people rate themselves as in very good health while in the local authority area in which it sits the percentage is 71.6 per cent but the national average is 68.8 per cent. Similarly, selecting housing shows you that in the same area 1.5 per cent of properties are empty and in the local authority area the number is 1.2 per cent while the average for England is 1.4 per cent. Despite its value for assessing the needs of the population, for demographic work and in the future for family and social history research, the future of the census is no longer assured and cheaper ways of obtaining the information are being discussed. The 2011 census could be the last to be conducted.

Using official statistics

If you are new to using statistics generally then you have to take care (irrespective of whether the statistics are official or not) about the interpretation and use of the figures. While statistics and statistical series can be very useful, they provide many traps for the unwary and those who are numerically inexperienced. The latter should not be put off, as a diligent and careful approach to the figures will often serve to replace mathematical or arithmetical ability. However, it is the unwary, the gullible, the reader in a hurry or the journalist pressed for a deadline who does not engage the brain before accepting the statistics who is likely to trip up.

When faced with a table of figures it is important not to panic. The figures will supply a particular set of data or support a particular hypothesis or conclusion. It is important not to lose sight of what you require and to ask if the numbers answer your needs or are the closest you can get. The checks to be made should include the following.

- *Source.* Is the source of the data authoritative and trustworthy? Are the figures compiled by an independent body or by an organisation with an axe to grind? Are you using the original source or a newspaper report or other secondary source of the data? Has someone given the figures a spin to advance his or her own ends? Check that the figures are official and don't rely on someone else to interpret the data for you. The source statement on the table may only give a broad indication of where the figures have come from, but it may be worth seeing if you can find more information and you may find that more detailed figures are available.

- *Methodology.* The method used to collect data affects their reliability and it is important to understand this before using statistics. Figures may be collected through sampling and the sample size used may vary. Crime figures, for instance, are based on reported crime and do not include crimes where the police have not been involved. The census is exceptional as it aims to canvass the total population.

- *Title.* It is important to look carefully at the title of the statistical table you are using to be certain it covers the exact subject for the data you seek.

- *Definition.* Look to see if there is a footnote that defines the content of the table more clearly than the title and shows what has been included or excluded to be sure it is what you need. What has actually been counted?

- *Comparing like with like.* When comparing different series, or figures from different years, check that they have been compiled on exactly the same basis, using the same definition. For example, when looking at an index with a base year that equals 100 and shows relative levels, check that tables use the same base year.

- *Unit of measure.* It is important to be sure you understand the units of measure being used in a table of statistics. A misunderstanding could lead to incorrect assumptions and wrong decisions being made. Is it a tonne or a ton? What currency is being used?

- *Dates covered.* Check that the data covers the years or months you need. Are there notes that warn that data for some years is more comprehensive than others?

- *Date of publication.* Check that you have the latest data available if that is what you require.

- *Geographical coverage.* It is essential to ensure you understand the geographical coverage of the data being used. Is it for England and Wales? Is Northern Ireland included?

Issues affecting official statistics

Statistics in any form can be difficult to employ and, although the digital age has made them easier to access, it has not necessarily made them easier to use.

There are very practical issues around the use of statistics. Even now, it is often easier for the lay person to use a printed rather that a digital source for statistical data. With digital sources the data appears as a string of numbers that can be difficult to interpret. In a print source the table will be clearly laid out with notes, footnotes and references to other tables. It is also easier to lay out several issues of a particular statistical table side by side for comparison. Apart from these physical practicalities there are a number of issues to consider when using official statistics.

Archiving

Access to older statistics is needed to be able to see how things have changed over time and what is available online will be at the most 15 years, worth. Print statistics, by comparison, have been available for two centuries. There is concern about the digital preservation of statistics. With the move to digital-only publication, a situation could be imagined where we fail to preserve the electronic version, there is no longer a print version and therefore a comparison over time becomes impossible. Is anyone scanning/digitising statistics collections?

Cost and time

Although official statistics are now mainly available free of charge on the web, they can be held within large files which take a considerable time to download. If the user needs to print them in order to use them successfully, this could be an expensive operation.

Trust

The consultation document *Independence for Statistics* published by the Treasury in 2006 set out the following key objectives for the reform of the statistical system:

- statistics should be of high *quality*, that is produced to the highest professional standards and fit for purpose;
- statistics should have high *integrity*, that is be free from political interference;
- roles and responsibilities should be clearly defined and mechanisms should be in place to hold the system to *account*.

To contribute to achieving these objectives the Statistics and Registration Service Act 2007 was passed and the UK Statistics Authority created in April 2008. As we have seen, it is 'an independent body operating at arms' length from Government as a non-ministerial department, directly accountable to Parliament'. Statistics are used to hold the government to account and it is essential therefore that official statistics are free from political interference and that the citizen can have faith in them. That is not to say that they can't be used in a political way to present the government in a favourable light.

Consistency

In using statistics, the current situation or the situation at a particular point in time may be required. However, more often than not you are seeking trend data which will show you how things are changing or have changed and the direction in which an activity is going. In order to see these, you need statistics which present the data consistently, and changes in the way they are collected or published will not help here. There may be changes to the title, sets of data are discontinued, responsibility may pass from one government department to another or a department may change its name. An example of this is the subject of housing which is covered in the case study below where there is a good example of government structural changes making data more difficult to find.

The Housing Corporation, for example, since its creation in 1964, had funded new affordable housing *and* had been the regulatory body for housing associations. In December 2008 it was replaced by the Homes and Communities Agency (HCA) (*www.homesandcommunities.co.uk*) as the national housing and regeneration agency for England and the Tenant Services Authority (*www.tenantservicesauthority.org*) as the regulatory body for Registered Social Landlords. The only statistics the HCA publishes are called National Housing Statistics but in fact they are simply statistics on the supply of affordable homes delivered under the National Affordable Housing Programme and so provide very limited statistics.

Housing statistics – case study

The government department responsible for housing is Department for Communities and Local Government (DCLG). The Department was created in 2006 and it covers areas of work previously the responsibility of:

- Department of the Environment (DOE);
- Department of the Environment, Transport and the Regions (DETR);
- Department of Transport, Local Government and the Regions (DTLR); and
- Office of the Deputy Prime Minister (ODPM).

The DCLG and its predecessors have a long history of collecting housing data, principally to inform government housing policy. They have tried, as far as is reasonably practical, to collect information in a fixed format over many years to facilitate longitudinal comparisons. This has been done through the principal annual publication, *Housing Statistics*. The range of statistics covered, their presentation and table numbering has remained fairly fixed over 30 years so users can easily access the latest results for long-term data series and make comparisons.

With the advent of online access to statistics, DCLG's website has continued to refer to its *Housing Statistics* publication, allowing free downloads of all the publication's tables from its website, while also continuing to make hard copies available to purchase. Users are taken straight to a menu of housing topics, asked to select a topic and are then offered a list of relevant downloadable tables, for example 'house building'. This approach avoids users having to know about the details of existing housing statistical publications, an advantage for new users.

The way DCLG presents online statistics allows them to include both data from their current publications and from other data sources, including non-governmental data. A three-figure classification applied to both departmental data and data from other organisations facilitates this approach. The tables in this classification are called 'live tables' as they are updated as fresh data becomes available. An index is provided.

To see how effective this approach is, a list of common housing statistics that a housing researcher might require has been drawn up to see how well they are covered by the system.

A typical selection might be:

1. *For the private housing sector:*
    (a) House building: annual new housing completion
    (b) House price levels (private sales)

    (c) Rent levels (private rented sector)

    (d) Numbers of tenancies (private sector).

2. *For the social housing sector:*

    (a) Rent levels (for council housing and for housing associations – Registered Social Landlords (RSLs))

    (b) Numbers of tenancies

    (c) Social housing annual repair costs (both day-to-day maintenance and major repairs)

    (d) Social housing annual management costs

    (e) Numbers of tenancies transferred from the council sector to the housing association sector (over the past 20 years in accordance with government policy on this issue)

    (f) Proportion of tenants claiming housing benefit.

1 Private housing

(a) House building: annual housing completions

The home page provides a link to 'Housing' – bear in mind that Communities covers a range of non-housing government responsibilities. A careful look at the housing web page reveals a further link to 'Research and statistics'. Following this link and selecting 'Housing statistics' rather than 'Housing research', the next page opens up to several options and these can be used either to learn more about the organisation of statistics by Communities or to search directly for the data of interest. By selecting 'Housing statistics by topic', the search 'House building' should be selected. The result is a link to 20 relevant 'live tables' all downloadable in Microsoft Excel format.

    The data in these tables provides extensive coverage of house building activity, with historic series by country, by region and by local authority district.

(b) House price levels (private sales)

Returning to the list of topics for which housing statistics are available, for house price data the obvious selection to make is 'Housing market and house prices'. Following the link to the downloadable live tables, several files are available including:

■ national house price levels from 1930 to the present (UK from 1970 to the present);

■ UK house prices, simple averages, by region, by type of buyer and by new/existing dwellings since the 1990s;

■ UK house prices, averages adjusted for mix of dwellings, by region, by type of buyer, and by new/existing dwellings since the 1990s;

■ house prices, mortgages and incomes of borrowers;

■ UK house price inflation, comparisons between DCLG data (from Council of Mortgage Lenders (CML)) with indices published by Halifax Building Society and Nationwide Building Society – Halifax and Nationwide data is seasonally and mix adjusted for dwelling types; CML data is not seasonally adjusted, only mix adjusted;

■ house price inflation compared with general inflation, plus data about numbers of transactions, mortgages and repossessions;

■ land price data for England and Wales from 1990;

■ house price data at local authority district level, available from the Land Registry for England and Wales since 1996.

From this list of data files there is potentially everything that would ever need to be known about house prices. The local authority level data, which was not previously available directly from the Communities website, is particularly useful and supplements the house price data at county level provided in the *Housing Statistics* publication.

One essential point from the data above is that statistics on official websites are not necessarily 'official'. The source of much of this data is the Council of Mortgage Lenders and reference is made to house price data published by the Nationwide and Halifax building societies.

(c) Rent levels (private rented sector)
To research this next topic, return to the list of topics where 'Rents, lettings and tenancies' is the obvious choice and provides a list of relevant live tables.

2 For the social housing sector:

(a) Rent levels (for council housing and for housing associations – RSLs)
Local authority rents at both regional and district level are provided and the district data is particularly useful as districts are responsible for the management of council housing and the rents charged. Data for local authority rents are collected by the finance division of Communities rather than by the statisticians and have only more recently been made available.

It is important to understand how data is collected in order to understand its limitations and the tables giving rents for properties operated by RSLs are a case in point. Data is collected by the Tenant Services Authority by asking RSLs to complete an annual Regulatory and Statistical Return and this is based on property for people with general needs. The figures collected and used are from the larger RSLs only. Until 2006 this applied to RSLs who owned or managed at least 250 units or bed spaces but from 2007 the number of units was increased to 1,000. The availability of RSL rents by local authority sector (adjusted to take into account the fact that some housing associations will extend across local authority boundaries) is very useful. The live tables available provide good coverage of information on rent levels for all tenures over the past ten years.

(b) Numbers of tenancies
For numbers of tenancies by tenure a further series of live tables containing data for stock and households is available by selecting the topic 'Housing stock'. 'Household estimates and projections' is the topic to select to look at forecasts for housing units by tenure into the future usually issued for the next 11 years.

(c) Proportion of tenants claiming housing benefit
This topic is an example of where you may find data on more than one government website but it may well be the same data. The proportion of tenants claiming housing benefit can be found on the Communities site by following the link to 'Rents, lettings and tenancies' through to live table 718 entitled 'Household units receiving housing benefit'.

This table will tell you the proportions of:

■ housing association tenants on housing benefit;

■ private rented sector tenants on housing benefit;

■ LA council tenants on housing benefit.

The figure given for the total number of local authority tenant benefit units is 1,310,000 and from the housing stock topic table 116 we learn that the total local authority tenant figure for England was 1,987,343 allowing calculation of the missing figure.

However, could this figure be obtained from the website of the Department for Work and Pensions (DWP)? The data is all there on the DWP site although it is not as easy to navigate as the Communities site. However, to be fair to DWP, they have considerably more data to present.

Conclusion

From the list of information identified at the beginning of this case study we find comprehensive coverage of much of what is needed and in particular:

- new house building: ten years' historical data down to regional and district level;
- house prices: ten years' historical data down to regional and district level, and longer series at national level;
- housing units/tenancies by tenure: ten years' historical data down to regional and district level;
- rent levels, both private and social rented sector: ten years' historical data down to district level.

In other areas such as social housing annual repair costs and for social housing annual management costs there is nothing for the private or the RSL sectors because the data is not collected. English aggregate LA council housing repair and management costs were available through the topic 'Housing finance' for each of the past ten years. Information concerning stock and tenancy numbers, house building, house prices and rents is plentiful, but for running costs, rent rebates and housing transfers it is more patchy.

Other sources of housing data

One of the strengths of the Communities system for accessing housing statistics is the inclusion within their system of data from non-DCLG sources, such as the Nationwide and

Halifax house price database and the DWP database of housing benefit data.

References

National Statistics (2000) *Framework for National Statistics,* First Edition, Operational from 2000. Online.

Pickford, Stephen et al. (1989) *Government Economic Statistics: A Scrutiny Report.* London: TSO.

9

The future of access to official information

The changes in the availability of official information since David Butcher published the second edition of *British Official Publications in Britain* in 1991 have been dramatic and rapid. There have been changes in the technology, in society and in government and it seems that these changes and the speed of change are set to continue. So what will this mean for the future of access to official information?

Information versus publications

One of the major changes is that the focus now seems to be on access to information rather than publications. When the Standing Committee on Official Publications (SCOOP) was formed forty years ago the focus was almost entirely on publications. As websites began to appear in the public sector the emphasis was still very much on how publications were made available through them. Perhaps since the implementation of the Freedom of Information Act and its requirement to make information available and with developments in digital technology, the emphasis has shifted from publications to information. Data files, tables and web content are now made available and these are not necessarily being brought together to form publications. We still have, of course, many well known and easily recognised publications such as *Hansard*, Select Committee reports, statistical publications, bills, acts, statutory instruments, consultation documents and many of the publications covered in this book. However, increasingly we are seeing the emphasis being placed on access to information as, for instance, with the government requirement for local authorities to publish details of all expenditure over £500, for central government to publish expenditure over £25,000 and in the open data agenda generally.

Open data has seen organisations encouraged to make data sets freely available for re-use in, for instance, 'apps' for mobile phones or for 'mashing up' with other data to provide an information tool such as *FIND's Personalise Your Map,* a freely available mapping tool. From the website at *www.findfreemaps.co.uk* public data from organisations such as Natural England and Ordnance Survey can be used on maps which can be annotated and saved as pdfs allowing users to create maps for a selected area and with the colours, style and data they require. This allows maps to be developed by individuals for very specific purposes and goes well beyond the facility that has been offered by Ordnance Survey for some time which was to provide a map centred on an individual postcode.

Another example of the high-profile publication of data is the crime statistics service provided at *www.police.uk* where an address or postcode search will provide you with a record of crimes in the area, names and contact details for local police officers, police stations and advice and information on crime and safety.

This approach to making data available means it can be disseminated quickly and easily but what it can lack is the structure, analysis and interpretation that would perhaps be included if the information were drawn together into a publication.

Open data is added to *data.gov.uk*, for instance, by a number of government departments but was listed with little structure and the data itself is in a fairly raw form. This is, of course, exactly what has been required as a way of encouraging serendipity in the approach to developing apps but is perhaps not ideal for anyone wanting to use that data in a more traditional way. The structure is improving with the use of tags and the ability to search quite effectively.

An example would be a search on a health topic. There are well over a thousand data sets listed so the task of finding something useful is a challenge. This is helped by subject tags and tags for publishers, format and nation which will allow you to filter the listings and search by keyword. Taking cancer survival rates as an example, a search by keyword turns up tables of survival for five years after diagnosis. The user is directed to related data sets for:

- cancer survival by Primary Care Trusts;
- cancer survival by Cancer Network;
- cancer survival in England by government office region, Strategic Health Authority and Cancer Network.

All the data sets on this particular topic are provided by the Office for National Statistics and appear on *www.statistics. gov.uk* so would have been available before the open data site was established. The data also has the advantage of having been collected over a long enough period for there to be comparative data and there are notes and explanation included.

Another example identified by looking at the data sets as published by a department is the Cabinet Office monthly lists of search terms used on the Directgov website. The lists date back to September 2010 when the most popular search term was 'student finance'. Unlike the example above, this is information which was not available previously and is in the form of an Excel spreadsheet with no interpretation or explanation.

Technology

We have moved from a time when a computer was a specialist tool for use in the world of work to something small enough and simple enough to use in the home, to the stage now where a computer is pocket sized, combined with a mobile phone and camera and more powerful than those used to control the space missions of the 1960s. It is carried with us at all times and gives us access to a wealth of information, it keeps us in touch with the world and family and friends, it stores our photos, acts as a satnav and gives us access to our email. We have seen it contribute in recent times to the bringing down of governments and it has been used to spread images of natural disasters faster than traditional broadcasting methods.

By 2011 Facebook had more than 600 million active users so has, in effect, a population twice the size of the USA. That makes it an incredibly powerful tool and it has been used, for instance, to orchestrate political unrest in the Middle East and alert the world to the devastation caused by the earthquakes and tsunami in Japan in 2011.

The hardware we use changes and develops so rapidly that last year's mobile looks dated but the developments in the software are, if anything, even more impressive. In the area of official information use is made of blogs, Facebook, Twitter, crowd sourcing, data mashing, podcasts, webcasting, YouTube, Flickr, SMS and other software to inform, consult and engage the public. Bookmarking is offered through Delicious, Reddit, Diff This, Newsvine, StumbleUpon and

Bebo. Links to all these will be found on public sector websites to a greater or lesser extent.

The developments in technology have led to an information revolution which has changed the way we manage information. A video on YouTube by Michael Wesch of Kansas University tracks this change from the time when information was in a book on a shelf and could be catalogued and classified. It was a 'thing' with a logical place. The video explains that information now has no material form and this forces us to rethink how we manage it. The final message of the video is that we all have responsibility for creating, organising, critiquing and harnessing information. Today a TV programme or radio show can be almost entirely created from information contributed by interested members of the public submitting ideas and questions. Crowd sourcing is the term used to describe the way the public can be used to create and manage information. The NetMums website is an example of a site where content is based on information contributed by mums for mums (not forgetting dads and others who care for children) (*www.netmums.co.uk*). Sites which provide reviews of hotels, books or domestic appliances use the same principle of people providing information from their own experience for the benefit of others. Of course, you can't always be sure that a bad review is not malicious and a good review not provided by someone with a vested interest and designed to drum up business.

Another example of an information resource developed from crowd sourcing is the snow map of the UK found at *www.uksnowmap.com* This website uses tweets on Twitter from people who tweet their location and the rate of snow falling on a scale of one to ten and the information is used to build up a map of snow conditions across the country.

What is expected of official information is that it will be accurate and trustworthy. If information is published in a document by a central government department it is assumed it has been written by experts and checked for accuracy and has the stamp of approval of the government. Crowd sourcing information, as with, for example, Wikipedia, NetMums and holiday or retail sites, means that there will be questions about the accuracy of the information provided. If anyone can add to or update the information there is, of course, a risk that they will add wrong or distorted information.

Society

Society too has changed and is changing and this cannot be separated from the information revolution. In the UK there is a digital divide and a need to ensure access for those without the skills and the technology, but there is now a generation who have grown up with a PC, laptop or notebook and a mobile phone and use them to manage their lives from keeping in touch with friends to submitting homework, from shopping to entertainment.

We have moved from needing to visit a library or reach for a set of encyclopaedias to check a fact or figure, to logging on to a PC and the Internet to use Google or Wikipedia, to using a smart phone to access this information in an instant wherever we are. When you spot someone on TV or in a film and can't remember what else they have appeared in you no longer have to scratch your head and try to remember. Google on your smart phone will provide the answer. Real-time information about train arrivals can be delivered directly to your mobile, letting you plan your travelling and avoid wasted time. Cameras and the ability to share images are standard parts of mobile telephones, allowing for the sharing of images instantly.

The number of adults in the UK shopping online has risen from less than 20 per cent in 2003 to 62 per cent by 2010 according to figures from Tesco Retailing Services, and the growth in food shopping is estimated to average 15.6 per cent each year up to 2014.

If society continues to develop in this way, as it makes use of the emerging technologies and the developing services made possible as a result, then pressure on all tiers of government to keep pace and make official information as readily available will also grow.

Despite the attempts to close the digital divide and encourage use of the Internet in particular, it is possible that as the technology develops the divide will become greater as those who could cope with the internet and email struggle to find a use for Facebook, Twitter and other social media tools.

Government

Consultation and engagement

Any government must change and adapt as society changes if it is to be responsive to the needs of the electorate. Society in the UK is now used to being engaged and consulted and to contributing information and will expect the same approach from government, both central and local. Provision must be made for this and developments using the available technologies will be needed to engage all areas of society, not forgetting those who would still prefer more traditional methods of consultation.

Petitions have long been used to draw attention to an issue and seek to influence a debate. This could be a national issue such as changes to the law on fox hunting or a local issue such as the plans to permit extraction of minerals or build an incinerator or new housing. In the digital age the e-petition has developed and often attracts large numbers of 'signatures'. At central government level e-petitions with 100,000 or more signatures will trigger a debate in Parliament. In local government, schemes for the management of petitions generally have been required since 2010 and the number of signatures required in order for there to be a debate has been set locally within the guidance issued. It is anticipated that the Localism Bill will have an impact on this area of engagement.

Accountability

The scandal surrounding MPs' expenses and the severe financial pressures on the country and the public sector have increased the demand for accountability. The public are no longer content to simply trust their elected representatives to know best and get it right, but demand to know what is being spent, how decisions are made and why.

A similar development is the public reading stage of the bill process in Parliament covered in Chapter 3 'Parliament at Westminster'.

Another example followed reports that local authorities were preventing people from blogging or tweeting in council meetings. The Department for Communities and Local Government issued a letter which set out the government's support for what it called 'citizen journalists'. The letter said 'Bloggers, tweeters, residents with their own websites and users of Facebook and YouTube are increasingly part of the modern world, blurring the lines between professional journalists and the public'. It went on to say that to discourage people from using tools such as these to reach a wider audience is 'potentially at odds with the fundamentals of democracy'.

The government response has been to make information available and the open data work in particular is designed to show the 'workings' as you would if tackling a maths problem and not just to provide a solution.

Publishing data is complex when services are provided by central government and by the various tiers of local government. The move to commission public services from private sector providers rather than delivering them directly may make this even more complex. It has been shown with, for example, the requirement to publish spending figures, that legislation, incentives and penalties are needed if full national coverage is to be achieved. Further legislation and enforcement may well be required if consistent and comprehensive data is to be made available in future.

Conclusion

This book has sought to explain how official information is made available today and how this has changed since the advent of the digital age. It has set out the structures and functions at each level of government and within the bodies which surround and support them. The aim has been to help the reader understand what the official bodies are, what information they publish, how it is published and how it can be exploited. It has sought to promote it as a rich vein of information which can easily be overlooked or seen as difficult to penetrate.

Official publishing is a rapidly changing area where every day brings new developments and new ways for people to access information which will help them understand the society in which they live, access the services they need and hold to account those who govern them. The transparency agenda set out by the Coalition government, the demands of society to be heard and involved in decision-making and the growing expectations of the public based on their experience of accessing information generally will continue to drive improvements in access to official information.

Keeping track of this valuable source of information will remain a challenge even if it is a very different one from the days of printed publications. It is, however, well worth the effort. It is a body of information, access to which is required by professionals in many specialist fields such as economists, scientists, engineers and those working in health services. However, perhaps more importantly it is essential information for the everyday use of the citizen of the UK in accessing services they need such as education and social care, paying their taxes, knowing, understanding and complying with the law of the land and and holding to account their elected representatives whether this be at local or central government level.

Index

Finding Official British Information

'reserved matters,' 104
Review of Sub-national Economic Development and Regeneration, 135–6
revised statutes, 76–7
Road Traffic Regulation Act (1984), 32, 34
Robbins, M., 1
Royal Assent, 71–2
Royal Letters Patent, 170–1
RSS feeds, 12–13

Science and Technology Facilities Council, 190
Scotland, 104–117, 184, 207, 221, 238–9
 further information, 114–15
 official online gateway, 116–17
 publications and information, 109–14
 regional development bodies, 138–9
 structure and functions, 105–14
 visiting Scottish Parliament, 115–17
Scotland Act (1998), 104
Scottish Arts Council, 184
Scottish Confederation of University and Research Libraries (SCURL), 117
Scottish Drug Enforcement Agency, 209
Scottish Enterprise, 139
Scottish Government, 108–9, 116
Scottish Information Commissioner, 5
Scottish National Party (SNP), 109

Scottish Parliament, 105–8
 Acts and Statutory Instruments, 113–14
 bills, 113
 committees, 106–8
 minutes of proceedings, 112–13
 other publications, 114
 publications, 173
Scottish Parliament *Annual Report*, 114
Scottish Parliament Bibliography, 114
Scottish Parliament Information Centre (SPICe), 110
Scottish Parliament Statistics, 114
Scottish Public Bodies Directory, 25
Scottish Statutory Instruments, 114
Scottish Working Group on Official Publications (SWOP), 117
search engines, 243–4
Second Reading, 68
Select Committee system, 77–83
 departmental select committees, 77–81
 general committees, 82
 Lords select committees, 81–2
 other committees, 82–3
 regional select committees, 82
Senedd, 126
Serious Fraud Office, 167
Serious Organised Crime Agency (SOCA), 209
Sessional Information Digest (SID), 52, 58–9
Shipman Inquiry, 29, 168
Shires south of the Tees, 214

CPSIA information can be obtained at www.ICGtesting.com
Printed in the USA
BVOW041307150112

280429BV00004B/5/P